Overcoming

Sales

Objections

Part Three

SALES TRAINING

Wayne E Shillum – Author

WES MARKETING

OVERCOMING SALES OBJECTIONS

Wayne E Shillum – Author

WES MARKETING

Dedication

3

To my discovery that Objections are not Bad after all

They are simply questions that need to be answered

Before the client will say yes

Table of Contents

INTRODUCTION

The process of "Overcoming an Objection" is really answering a question or concern that a prospect has, that is preventing you from continuing with the selling process.

Many people new-to-sales consider Overcoming Objections to be trickery, and they could not be farther from reality.

Knowing the fundamentals of answering an objection is a sales person's way of eliminating the obstacles that are continuously being placed in their pathway to the order.

Knowing how to handle objections will clarify one's message and allow them to continue with a presentation.

If left unanswered the client will build resistance to the sales effort and they may end the process, before the full message can be delivered.

Conditions

There are also obstacles known as conditions. A Condition is a real reason for the customer not purchasing a product or service.

They can be either permanent obstacles or temporary.

Many times, objections are presented as conditions. One will need to know how to establish if it is a real reason why the prospect cannot buy, or if it is information they need before they will proceed.

Misunderstood

The greatest misunderstanding of objections in the sales process is that they are often viewed as bad things, a prospects final answer, a final rejection, or the loss of opportunity; when they are only questions that need answers.

All prospects resist being sold something; but most will buy something they want or need. They will invest in those benefits or solutions, if the roadblocks are removed by answering their concerns.

Defense

Objections are defense mechanisms that are often used spontaneously by the client, to resist an unsolicited approach or the making of any decision to purchase something.

They can also just be indicating a need for clarification or a request for more information. The greatest mistake is to treat objections as bad things and something to be afraid of.

Objections are often buying signals that provide the seller with the keys to what will make the prospect purchase their offerings.

Once the sales person treats objections in this manner they will no longer fear an objection.

They will look for the hidden message and get excited when an objection occurs.

Vulnerability

Objections often indicate a prospect's vulnerability when they are presented with an idea, asked a question or asked to purchase one's offerings.

They are indeed roadblocks when this happens; and they are used to slow down the momentum of the sales effort, to avoid drifting into a commitment that the prospect may not want to make, at that time.

There are five steps to answering an objection. These steps will allow one to clarify the objection (question) and provide a way to find the right answer for the prospect's hesitation.

It is impossible for us to provide examples of every objection that might occur; but, we have separated and provided common groupings that objections will fall into.

Answering Objections is a necessary skillset to find out what is holding the Prospect back from going any further. Your job will be to hear them out and answer their concerns.

When Objections Occur

Knowing how to handle objections is very important in the selling process because objections can come at anytime and anywhere in your discussions.

You do not even need to be asking for an order to find the need to handle an objection.

First Contact

An objection can come from a first contact in your prospecting efforts simply because many people dislike the intrusion or interruption of their daily routine.

Often as soon as you start talking about your offerings and ask some questions you will be met with objections.

Objections are rejections of what is being presented, how something is presented or when it is presented. They can also give the prospect time to think.

Their first reaction Often

Is simply to *Object to the Intrusion*

Knowing how to respond to their objection can give you a second chance to be heard.

Objections are the roadblocks that stand between, where you are in the selling process; and your goal to find a need, make an appointment, qualify a prospect, or make a sale.

Objections can come during a first meeting, fact finding meetings, when you are making your final presentations and when you ask for the order.

When Closing the Sale

Overcoming or Answering Objections is the other half of the Dynamic Duo in the Closing Process. It is also the completion of the Closing Process.

Once you have mastered *"Closing the Sale" and" Overcoming Objections" (the Dynamic Duo),* you will be ready to fully appreciate and use your Prospecting skills and Sales Presentation skills.

Prospecting and Sales Presentations appear to come before this "dynamic duo" in the selling process.

And yes, the first thing you may be doing is prospecting; but, you will need both dynamic duo skills to achieve any kind of success in Prospecting or making Sales Presentations.

"Overcoming Objections," will be required from the moment you start your selling efforts, and it will be used right to the very end when you are securing the order.

Wrong Concept

The time for answering objections is often viewed by many as something only required at the very end of a selling presentation, where the sales person has asked for the order.

This is indeed a moment when one will surely get objections, but it is not the only time that they will be presented and need to be addressed. You can expect to be met with objections the minute you begin talking to your prospects.

If you want to be successful in your sales efforts, you must be ready to answer these earlier objections the moment that you start your conversations.

The Five Steps

There is a proper way to answer objections and you will need to know the five main steps to do it properly.

Our Approach to Answering Objections

- We show these five steps and how to use them.
- We show you how to change a condition into an objection and then how to solve it for the sale.
- We show you the bad words you should not use
- We show you the right words to replace them.
- We provide examples for the different types of objections and the ways to answer them

The examples we provide might not be the type of sales that you find yourself in; but, the concept for solving them, is what we are showing.

The expertise of overcoming objections is not trickery but an absolutely required skill in your professional sales tool kit, to be successful in selling.

The ability to answer objections will provide you with the confidence to be able to say (when you get and objection):

Great - an Objection

This will be one of the items

They will base their Buying Decision on

This Sale can be mine if I answer it right

OBJECTIONS OR CONDITIONS

The Definitions

The Dictionary Defines OBJECTION as follows:

- A comment or reason offered in opposition,
- A refusal or disapproval
- A feeling of dislike or disagreement
- A protest, a feeling of hostility or Doubt

Our Definition of OBJECTION

An Objection is a Question that is based on a customer's lack of understanding or insufficient information. It is a legitimate reason for not moving forward or buying at that time.

The Dictionary Defines a CONDITION as follows

- A state of a person or thing
- A modifying circumstance
- A prerequisite

Our Definition of a CONDITION

A Condition is a reason for not buying that exists.

Conditions can be temporary or permanent. They are legitimate reasons that will prevent prospects from being able to purchase your product or service.

Why Objections Happen

The Prospects Right to Object

It is the prospects right to object to an untimely or poorly presented prospecting call, a badly presented idea, a misleading comment or any excessive pressure for an answer or commitment to buy.

It is the right of the prospect to "Object" to making a purchase" or "Question it," if someone is trying to close, and the prospect is still not happy with all of the facts at hand.

It is their Right to Object

To any Information that is Not Clear

Where do Objections Occur?

As previously mentioned, they occur everywhere along the way from first contact to the end.

Many attempts to approach a client in the beginning and throughout one's dealings with them; right up to the end, may be met with conditions, objections or questions.

They become extremely critical items to solve; for the sales person, in the final stages of obtaining the sale.

Unless you know how to handle these objections correctly, you will stumble and fall before you reach the finish line. Knowing how to answer objections is like putting the icing on the *"Sales Cake."*

This part of the selling process will provide closure to each part of your mission.

By learning the reasoning (the why) behind our answers to objections, you will acquire a key component of your closing tool kit. Understanding the "why" gives you flexibility and depth in your ability to handle the many different situations that will arise.

Different Groups for Objections

Our "Answers to Objections" will fall into distinctive groups. Recognizing a group, will allow you to use a similar response for each group.

In each group, you will need to change the ingredients to suit the situation, but you will always find a common ingredient in that group that allows you to select your answer.

Our Six Main Groups

1) Preventable Objections
2) Price Objections
3) Competition
4) Change of Base
5) What Would You Do
6) Conditional Objections

The Importance of Understanding the Why

In the beginning one might think there are just too many ways to answer objections and they get frustrated and confused.

Fortunately, after learning our methods and examples, a pattern should emerge, and our groupings will make sense.

It is not our intent to present the following examples as a script in a play to be learned and recited verbatim.

The memorizing of our example responses is intended to embed the concepts in one's subconscious.

The final wording and presentation should become that of the individual and not the teacher.

Once the conceptual part of the process is learned and understood the presenter (sales person) will have unlimited scope in the ability to overcome objections.

It is our intent to leave you with an understanding of what is behind all these groups and different responses.

What We Want to Happen

Learning the WHY is important, because it gives one the ability to handle almost everything that will be thrown at them in the selling process.

CONDITIONS

What ae Conditions?

Conditions exist because of circumstance. They are different from objections because the prospect has a legitimate reason for not buying and it exists.

Objections are often Presented as Conditions

Sales people will often believe what has been presented is an actual reason that is preventing the Prospect from making a purchase.

Whether Condition or Objection, it is a roadblock created by the prospect that is presented to avoid deciding.

A Condition Always Needs to be Challenged

Conditions do exist and once they are discovered to be an actual condition, they become a justifiable reason for not making a purchase.

It may be time to move on to the next lead or find out if it is temporary, long term or permanent.

Examples of Conditions:

- No money, no credit, too sick to carry on
- Price is totally over our budget (for real)
- Need to talk to Someone who is not there
- I am waiting for all the prices to come in
- Product is too big for the space available
- No need. No possible use for it

Handling Conditions and Objections

Treat Everything as an Objection

It is important to understand the difference between a condition and an objection. It will also be your responsibility to challenge what has been presented as a condition.

As already mentioned, many reasons presented as conditions are really an excuse for not buying. They are not conditions but perhaps procrastination hidden behind a condition.

The First Time you hear a Condition:

- Acknowledge the condition that they have presented.
- Then continue (by pass it).

If it is a real condition, they will bring it up again and it may be a real condition.

- If it isn't a condition; but an objection, and the condition doesn't exist, and you have accepted it as a condition, **you lose.**
- If you do not challenge it and fail to continue to qualify and use your skill set for handling objections, **the prospect has won.**
- If it is only an objection; and you do not get a potential order, it's your fault and **you have failed in your mission.**

When you have listened to the reason (condition) given by the prospect outlining why they cannot proceed, you must always challenge it.

The Situation

A customer's condition, objection or question is what we refer to as a request to get further information, or solve an issue, before they (the prospect) will proceed further.

The Mission

You will need to find out exactly what the condition or objection is, answer if fully to their satisfaction, before you can expect the client to proceed. Very few sales occur without having to answer an Objection.

Their Right to say No

The prospect has every reason to expect and get everything they need to make them comfortable with what you are asking them to do.

Your answers to the prospect should give them the information they are asking for. This knowledge is what they need to solve their concerns. Your answer should remove the concern and the objection.

If the information or answer is not good enough, then you will need to continue the process until you have fully answered all their questions and removed all their concerns.

Your Right to Continue

Once you have answered their objections, it is then your right to expect an okay to continue, or the right to ask for an order from them.

When closing a sale, you should always finish your answers to an objection with the request to proceed or for an order.

At the very least, expect a confirmation that you have answered their question and they are satisfied with the answer.

Continue this process throughout your prospecting, your meetings, sales presentation, and your closing attempts until the customer says yes to your final request for an order.

Asking a Prospect to Purchase

Before you have Provided all their Answers

Is like

Expecting a Campfire to give you More Heat

Before you put Wood on it

Objections are Good!

Look for objections or questions, for they are the things that are important to your client, and they are ultimately the reasons that will cause them to go ahead or reject the possibility of an order.

When you hear an objection, get excited because often they are positive signs and show interest. Say to yourself this is great because this may be a reason why, they will buy

Mastering the skill set of *"overcoming objections"* will help you unravel what the prospect is really thinking and show you the way to get the order.

A right answer puts things into a proper prospective for everyone.

Changing Conditions to Objections

Often you will be presented with objections in the form of conditions and below are some examples of conditions that are really objections, that we will cover in more detail later.

1. Alternative viewpoint - Change of Base – *Time not Distance*
2. What would You Do – *That's what we did*
3. Need to Talk to Someone – *Let's call them or go see them*
4. Call back Objection – *Just leave the information*

The Customer is Always Right!

When you are presented with a condition or an objection:

- Do not disagree
- Do not argue
- You are not there to prove them wrong
- You are there to prove them right.

Proving them right is what will make them want to work with you and purchase your products or services.

Proving them wrong will prove why they should not be talking to you, and they should give the order to someone else!

First Part to Handling Objections

If someone throws a punch, do you normally step into it?

NO! – I hope not!

Not unless you want to be knocked out before you get started, or you wish to experience some damage or pain.

So why; when most sales people hear an objection, the first thing they do, is to jump right in and fight it?

They throw themselves right into the line of fire and challenge it.

Is that ever a BIG mistake!

What is the best way to avoid the damage of a punch?

- You step back,
- Or step aside
- And you roll with it.

Every time you hear an objection for the first time.

Step Back

> **You Say:** *"I understand your point of view"*
>
> Or
>
> *You Say: "I understand"*
>
> Or
>
> *You Say: "I can see why you feel this way"*
>
> **Step aside**
>
> You say: *"By the way"* and carry on with the presentation
>
> **You Roll with it**

By continuing with your presentation; if the objection is real, it will come up again.

If it is a real Objection

If the SAME objection comes up again, it probably is a legitimate Objection or maybe even be a Condition. This time you do not by-pass it.

The next five steps are critical to Determining Conditions or Overcoming Objections.

If you skip any of them, you will usually not finish this part of the process successfully.

THE RIGHT WAY TO HANDLE OBJECTIONS

We have already mentioned there are five steps to handle an objection or condition. Most new-to-sales people and many experienced sales people do not know the proper way to handle objections.

They fear these roadblocks because they do not understand that if an objection or condition occurs, it can be a good thing.

When an objection occurs, you have just been issued a warning by your prospect, that you need to explain something further or correct it.

If you know how to approach either an objection or a condition, there is no reason to panic. In fact, these warnings can often be a buying signal; the solution to which, is their reason to buy.

The following five steps are a tried and proven way to remove the roadblocks, so you can continue your journey.

Use These Five Steps

Clarification Part

  Step 1 – Question it

  Step 2 – Shut up and Listen!

  Step 3 – Confirm their Answer!

Solution Part

  Step 4 – Answer their Concerns!

  Step 5 – Confirm your Answer!

Steps 1, 2 and 3 usually follow the same approach. The Changes occur in the solution part Steps 4 & 5.

Once you Confirm your Answer - Carry on with the process

Or Ask for the Order

Clarification Part

Step 1) Question It

- Ask them to explain what they are Objecting to
- They will either start to explain and realize it is a stupid reason, or in explaining it, you find out their real objection or if it is a condition.

Step 2) Shut up and Listen

- Here them out
- Even if you think you know where they are going with the objection

SHUT UP AND LISTEN

Even if you guess right, you will probably upset them

And you could guess wrong!

Step 3) Confirm Their Answer

You Say: *"Just to confirm my understanding of why you feel this way?"*

Outline your understanding of the Objection or condition as they have explained it to you.

Solution Part

Step 4) Answer Their Concerns

- When you know what they are objecting to
- Provide your solution or answer to it - completely and thoroughly.

Step 5) Confirm Your Answer

You Say: *"Now that should answer your concern, am I right?"*

By following this proven format, you will have the greatest chance of discovering the real objections and answering the prospects concerns or you will learn that it is a condition.

This format is used in all our methods to answer objections and conditions.

When combined with your closing questions and main closes you will take control of your prospecting and your sales presentations.

You will know where you are headed always, how to get there and what to do when you get there.

When the Objection is fully Answered

Continue

Or

Ask for the Order

Other Bad Words

How often do you use the following words?

When you say these words, you create resistance, because they present the negative side to a sale.

Do not ask them to:

BUY – They have bought enough already.

PAY – They are already paying too much.

These words imply hardship or an obligation.

Ask them to:

INVEST! – They are getting something back from an investment.

OWN – When you own something it implies pride of ownership.

Do not ask for a DOWN PAYMENT – That sounds like a bad thing.

Ask for an INITIAL INVESTMENT: They are starting something good.

Do not Say: MONTHLY PAYMENT – They hurt. People hate monthly payments. They have too many already.

Call it – A MONTHLY INVESTMENT - They are much easier to deal with and this implies good things are happening.

Do not Refer to it as a: PURCHASE – They do not want to make purchases

Call it: AN INVESTMENT - They do not mind making investments

SOLD - They do not want to be sold.

     SOLD is only good if you are selling their house.

SELL - They do not want you to sell them something.

SELLING PRICE – Selling & Price are negative and obstacles.

Use the amount to OWN – People like owning things.

Use when you OWN – Something to look forward to

The Strangest Thing People do not like to:

BUY

PURCHASE

PAY

Be SOLD SOMETHING

BUT, THEY WILL *ACT*

***TO OWN* SOMETHING!**

Bad Phrases

This occurs a lot in retail sales and it is very annoying. You are checking out with your selected items at the cashier.

They Say: *"Is that all?"* or *"Is that it?"*

Your mental reaction: *"Are you not happy with my business. Do you think it is not enough? Are you expecting More?"*

How many times have you experienced this?

The right way

One should ask: *"Is there anything else I can help you with"*

Or

"Did you find everything you were after?"

How many people fail to show their appreciations for your purchase with these bad phrases   Maybe you are upset to the extent of going elsewhere in the future.

Sales Pitch, Spiel

Have you ever heard a sales person use these words? After I am finished my sales pitch/spiel, we will discuss that question.

- Pitches are what people with trench coats on the street corners make.
- They are what the criminal element of our business does.
- Spiel – that sounds like a con job to me.
- Your clients do not want to listen to pitches or spiels, but, they will listen to a Presentation

Sign Something

- Do not ask people to sign something.

- How many times are we told not to sign anything?

Don't sign anything until your lawyer looks at it. **Sign** is a bad word - yet it is used all the time.

OK or Approve

- Ask them to OK something or APPROVE it.

- It's strange, they will OK it or APPROVE it,

- BUT they will not SIGN it!

They do not need a Lawyer to - OK it or APPROVE it.

Contract

- How many times have you been asked to sign a contract?

- What have you been told about a contract?

The Warnings about the word Contract

- Watch out, be careful, and beware.

- Read it very carefully.

- Take it to a Lawyer or you will end up in court

They will not SIGN a CONTRACT
BUT
They will OK an AGREEMENT

Trade Terms

Every Industry has them, and too many people use them when they are talking to their customers. Often, they do it to show off.

Trade terms are OK, if you are talking to someone in your industry, because they are used by all the people in your trade or company. People in your trade or your industry understand what you are talking about.

Have you ever heard of radio sales people who are selling spots?

- My lawn has bare spots. I have enough of them.

- When my carpet gets a spot, I need to get it cleaned. I do not want any more spots.

It could be, when we finish your pro-forma.

- ○ Maybe the client knows what you mean,
- ○ Maybe, they are not quite sure.

If they do not understand, or are not quite sure, they will doubt you, and they will not buy from you.

Forget the Trade Terms - Use People Language

2 – Built-In Objections

Overview

If you know that your company, product or service has a built-in objection or even several of them; do not live in fear during your entire presentation, waiting for it/them to surface.

Most Companies Have them.

They are there just waiting to knock you off your feet. You feel that your client is waiting to hit you with one or all of them, so you begin to concentrate on how you will fight them off when they finally come.

You Lose your Focus

And the Impact of your Presentation.

How to Overcome it

Do not wait for it. Do not waste all your time waiting for it to happen; because, *"IT WILL HAPPEN."* It will usually happen just when you are describing your biggest selling feature, or you are about to close.

BANG! It hits you right between the eyes.

Brag about it. Make it a Feature

You will know what these things are, because they are part of the things that will drag your presentation down, and start you defending yourself, instead of selling your product or company

1. Terms and Conditions - Example

Let's say it is your ten pages of the clauses in your terms and conditions, that every one of your competitors is telling your clients about.

It is not a secret that most people hate a lot of *"small print"* when dealing with an important undertaking.

If your terms and Conditions are at all lengthy, you can expect this to be used against you.

You must turn this seemingly negative condition into a positive one.

Do not avoid talking about it because your competition almost certainly is. Even if they are saying nothing, your prospect is having a negative reaction, just looking at your 10 pages.

Your Competition may be saying: *"You should see their terms and conditions section."*

"Talk about fine print. It is 10 pages long. Our terms and conditions section are only one page and is simple and straight to the point."

Or

Your Client is mentally comparing it with your competitor's simple terms and conditions and starting to feel very uncomfortable.

Before your Prospect Hits you with any Criticism:

You say: *"You know our company has discovered that most people want to be comfortable in their working arrangement with another person or company."*

"We have recognized that this feeling is very much a concern with most of the people we talk to about using our service or our product."

"We are proud of what we have done about it."

Continue:

"We have put together a detailed list of the things, which we will do for our clients."

"We provide a complete description of our product and service."

"There is no second guessing about what is not there."

"We show and explains everything that we can possibly think of, that our customer wants to see and needs to know."

Emphasize this one: *"We do not Hide things"*

Continue:

"People do not like surprises especially ones that end up costing extra dollars at the end of the transaction."

"We are proud that our company has taken the time to outline full product descriptions and show a complete list of terms and conditions and explain them in detail."

Continue: "We fully Explain:"

"What we do, and what the customer needs to do"

"They are totally spelled out; so, there is very little chance of a misunderstanding during, or at the end of the project."

"If there is an issue, it is visible and can be addressed in advance, and solved before the order is placed."

"We know that when we present our proposal to our clients, they have all of the facts right up front."

"There is no reason to be afraid of what has not been said or not been written."

*"**COMPETITION** often leaves things out or hides them; which can result in many grey areas or questionable items in their quotations."*

"They are often able to show a considerably lower price because these things have not been said or shown."

*"Their **not included items** go unnoticed, and it is often too late when the EXTRA COSTS OCCUR."*

The Reasons

"We have found that what we show is the kind of information that all good managers today feel they need to be well informed in their decision-making process."

"That is why we have done this."

The Close

"Do you not agree that what we have done is a real benefit in your decision-making process?"

What Have You Just Done?

Can they now object to your 10 pages of terms and conditions? If they do, then they are saying that they are not a good manager.

Make this an entire up-front presentation of your terms and conditions.

Write your own version, memorize it, and rehearse it until you can deliver it with emphasis and enthusiasm. Choose how and when you introduce your explanation to suit the circumstances.

Continue with your Presentation or Your Close

Your company may not have a Terms and Conditions issue, and many do not. This is just an example of a built-in objection just waiting to happen.

2. Product is too Small - Example

Very often people relate size with ability to get something accomplished faster or better.

It is therefore not surprising that competitors will use this idea to discredit your product if it happens to be smaller than theirs.

You know your competition will probably say that your product is too small and maybe they will infer that the smaller size will negatively affect performance.

Your prospect may be thinking this very same thing when they look at it and compare it to the size of others.

That is Why

You must Immediately Turn the Size - Into a Benefit

You Say:

"Before I start; may I say that as a company, we are proud of the fact that we have a product that is smaller than most.

"Not only can it still provide everything that is expected of it, it can provide even more benefits than some of our competitor's larger products."

"They may imply otherwise because of size."

Continue:

"We offer something that will reduce the foot print required by normal equipment while providing the same, or even slightly better performance."

"It is our belief that size should not the issue!"

"One should be asking instead - can this product achieve what I need it to do in my (manufacturing or work environment?")

Finish by saying:

"I am sure you will agree that it is performance, not size that you are looking for. Am I right?"

Continue with your Presentation or Your Close

3. Company is too Young or too New – example

Every company has a beginning. Very often a new company will have a younger management team than their established competitors.

This is a very easy target; and something that many salespeople highlight when speaking about your company, if you are new or management is young.

There is no benefit in trying to outrun the inevitable road block because it will surface eventually.

If you let it happen on its own; it will then be a negative situation, because you will be defending the accusations of newness and lack of experience.

The best approach is to turn it into a positive situation by bringing it up first.

Before the client can say it

You say: *"Many people might think that our company is too new, or our management is too young; but, we are proud of our wealth of knowledge, and the vibrant energy that our young company has."*

Continue:

"As a company, we are not hampered by bad habits, or ruts that time can often create. We are excited about what we bring to the table, and the benefits that our company has to offer a company such as yours."

"Our management team is proud of their leading-edge technology, and their energy and ability to get the job done, quickly and properly."

"Is that not what really counts?"

If this is your company, write your version of this and memorize it. Practice it to perfection, so you can deliver it with enthusiasm.

Continue with your Presentation or Your Close

Note: This approach can be altered to suit *"too old"* as well and many other situations. "Too old becomes experienced"

4.Better Product or Service – Creates a Higher Price

If your company has higher quality offerings with more benefits and features, it will often mean higher prices.

If your design or engineering department does not cut corners to achieve a better Price; while competition does.

Make this a Feature and Benefit

Brag about it

Establish early that you may not have the lowest price at the end, but your clients do not unknowingly suffer with:

- Offerings that do not meet performance expectations

- Premature failures

- Improper Service or back up

- Warranties that are not honored

Qualify right up front and ask if they are willing to sacrifice the above for the lowest Price.

Summary of Built in Objections

These are only four examples of built in objections.

Every company has them and your competition is almost guaranteed to present them to your potential customer.

They might even be referred to as skeletons in your closet, mistakes, shortcoming's or failures.

It is essential that you review everything about your company and its offerings; that can be presented by your competition *negatively*, in their efforts to create negative reactions or doubts with your client.

Do not Run from Them

Because they will Always Be There.

You Must

1) Face them

2) Make them benefits

3) Brag about them

4) Explain why your company is proud of these facts

5) Use them in your introduction meeting and in your presentations and when you are closing.

If you're that proud of them - How can they be bad?

The Biggest Mistake

You Start Thinking:

- Why should I even bring these items out into the open?

- Maybe my competition is not even saying anything.

- Maybe my prospect is not thinking this way.

- By bringing these things out into the open, I might be harming my own chances.

Wrong! – In this kind of Reasoning

- You will still live in fear that prospect will present them

- You will lose your focus and control of your presentation.

- If your competition is aggressively after the order, they will very often do whatever it takes to get it.

- Built in Objections are real.

- Your Prospect can also see them, without help from others.

Take Control

Present Things Your Way

The Best Defense is Always a Good Offense!

PRICE OBJECTIONS

Overview

Pricing is the largest area where objections occur. There are many reasons for the variance in prices offered.

Companies will position themselves based on either 1 or 2

1. Providing quality offerings and proper servicing of client needs
2. Providing the lowest price and sacrificing quality and service

Some Reasons for Higher Prices

Bad Reasons for a Higher Price

1. Product Sourcing – too many middlemen, inefficient suppliers
2. Their Company Overhead – extravagant facilities and expenses
3. Company Profit Margins – too high to meet 1 and 2
4. Operating/manufacturing methods – inefficient, outdated
5. Delivery – their own is inefficient or they use outside sourcing where costs are too high

If you are the owner, you will always be faced with the problem of being too high for the "Bad Reasons" unless these items are resolved.

If you are the Sales Representative and these problems are not resolved, you will always be faced with this pricing issue. Perhaps you should look for a different employer.

Some Good Reasons for Being Higher

1. Your Product – Offers more features and Benefits, saves energy, provides lower operating costs or is more operator friendly and easier to use.
2. Service – Better equipped, more trucks, 24/7 availability, quicker response times, proven track record of dependability.

As the sales person or owner, you will need to show why your prices are higher for the "Good Reasons"

Prices can be lower because of the following reasons.

Bad Reasons for a Lower Price

1. Product Design or Quality – Poor design, corners cut for price
2. Product Service Quality – Poor to meet price, not dependable
3. Warranty – No ability or intention of providing it

If this is your Competition, you need to know about it. You need to find ways to effectively overcome prices that are lower for these bad reasons.

Good Reasons for Lower Prices

1. Company Sourcing – Excellent and cost effective
2. Company Overhead – Efficient and cost effective
3. Company Profit Margins – Effectively priced to sell
4. Company Manufacturing – Efficient and cost effective
5. Company Shipping – Good sourcing or have their own trucks with cost efficient delivery controls.

These reasons should become selling features of your company. There is nothing wrong with being lower for these reasons.

Make the above features part of every presentation

In working with your Prospect, you can:

1. Establish quality and performance as the clients most important criteria and continue your journey and use your benefits and features to out-sell your competition.
2. Maintain your pricing. Emphasize what problems the prospect may be inviting or what they will be giving up, if they choose only based on the lowest price.
3. Emphasis your benefits and quality and try to come close enough to your competition's price to get the order.
4. Recognize that price is all the prospect wants and move on.

Prices can Also Appear Unnecessarily High because of:

a) Your Incorrect Qualification of Clients Needs

In this case you must improve your process of qualifying and establishing your client's needs.

b) A Poor Presentation, where Value of your Offerings is not Seen

In this case, you must improve your presentation to show value of product or service (or both). You might need to add more enthusiasm or add better content and examples.

Point out features like

- Extended life of products (cost reduction)
- Lower Energy or Process Costs
- Space Savings, time savings
- Environmentally Friendly, less noise
- Much easier to operate, happier employees
- There are many more which will relate to one's offerings

If this seems difficult, you probably do not know your competition's offerings well enough (or even your own) to show the value-added features of your offerings.

There will almost always be objections to price as it is every purchaser's quest to get the best price possible.

Even when they are looking at what they know is the best value for their investment, the client will often still object to price.

As a company or the sales representative for a company one should always make allowance for this normal behaviour of a purchaser.

Be Prepared

This is an Inherent "Price Trait" of a Buyer

General Trends

- Emphasis on price seems to follow the state of the economy.
- When times are good, and the economy is strong, price seems to be second to quality, performance, benefits and service.
- When times get tough; purchasers still want the same quality, service and other amenities, but more emphasis is placed on price.

- Outwardly price will always take a prime considered position regardless of economy status.

All companies want products or services that have added value; and they often say price is most important, even though performance, service and quality is what they are mostly after.

If there appears to be little difference in quality, benefits, service or performance, price most often wins.

There is always more Loyalty in a Strong Economy

Those who service the prospect well and give the best advice, are often given the advantage position in consideration of any order.

Often the profitability of the prospects company itself; and the type of offerings it brings to the marketplace, will influence their decision.

Wherever a prospects own quality, price and performance level is; will often determine how they view the importance of these areas in a supplier.

How can they Focus on the Lowest Price?

If they Sell *"Value Added"*

This reference can also be a good example to use in answering any price objections.

No matter how strong or weak the economy is, or how profitable the company is; most purchases will still stress price, as being high on the requirement side of things.

To do otherwise; would be a big mistake and invite higher costs for the products or services they are considering.

Price will Often Determine Quality

Price often determines the quality of the offerings and it will be up to the sales people to show this and justify a higher price.

Every purchaser wants the best that their money can buy, without paying an unjustified premium to get it. They do not want to become victims of *"supplier greed."*

The purchaser also knows that price is often an indicator of what they will get, and it is up to the sales person to justify a higher price by showing:

- More benefits,
- Better quality
- Better performance
- Better warranty and service back up

Competition and Branding

You will be competing against companies that have achieved a better image due to their advertising, branding and past performances.

Often this can Justify their Higher Prices

You may have equaled their offerings in all the areas we have mentioned but may have a difficult time getting the order without offering a lower price to tip the scales.

This is when your own Good Marketing

And company's Past Performances can pay off

Make your company stand out in an area such as service, quality or performance to make the difference. Show that you do have more to offer.

Provide testimonials and references to show that your company is reliable and provides everything you say it does.

Lower Prices Achieved by Cutting Corners

You will compete against companies who use price as their greatest selling feature. They cut corners in quality and performance to achieve the best price.

Often purchasers are unable to see where or when this is happening, and you must find a discrete way in your qualification questions and presentations to show why the competitor's prices are lower.

Learn everything you can about your competition. Where are they positioned as far as quality, benefits, service, performance and price?

Find out how and where they cut these corners

Prepare Yourself

Build an Inventory of rebuttals for price comments.

You can subtly place them in all your presentations from your first meeting and along the way.

Do not just place them at the end when you are trying to get the order, or it may be viewed as mudslinging and unethical.

Along the way, they become fact

At the end, they will seem like Excuses

Use your mini-closes and answers for objections to find out where the prospect is placing the importance of price in their requirements.

Part of the selling process is conditioning your client for what you are going to ultimately present to them. You must show why it is their best choice and why it is better than what your competition will offer.

If they can visibly see all the benefits and features of your offerings, then price often will not become the main criteria for their decision. It will also not be a big surprise to them at the end.

The Inventory of Price Rebuttals

Use Phrases such as:

- A fair price allows the seller to provide the benefits, quality and performance, warranty and service back up that their clients are usually looking for.

- When price is the main or only criteria for measurement, then quality, service and performance will certainly suffer.

- The excitement of the lowest price ends when the offerings fail to provide what the purchaser expected and needed.

- Many sellers hide behind price to avoid providing quality and performance and eventually service.

- The lowest price often can only be achieved by cutting corners and providing inferior products or services.

- The lowest price is not always the best choice when it comes to benefits and performance or honoring a warranty.

- We ask for a fair price; because it allows us to deliver what the customer needs in performance, benefits and quality - while still providing excellent service and full warranty.

- What are you ultimately after; the lowest price, or products and services that provide what you want and need at a competitive price.

- It is easier for a company to offer the lowest price if they have no intention of standing behind their offerings for service or warranty.

- Are you simply after the best price?

Keep adding to this list and make it as-long-as possible.

REMEMER the good reasons for offering a lower price. It is why you have it. Always stress these reasons for being able to offer it.

How to Handle Price Objections

First Encounter with a Price Objection

This will usually happen when you have finished your presentation and you have just provided your price.

You may not have even tried to make your final close and the client is already objecting to price. Often it is just their normal way of treating all prices.

They say: *"Wow! your price is too high!"*

When This Happens

The first time you hear it, acknowledge it and by pass it.

You say: *"I understand how you feel*

Bypass it and Start or Continue your Close

If you try to finish or try to close the sale and the objection or condition is real, they will repeat their earlier comment that the price is too high

Second Encounter with a Price Objection

The prospect might Say *"This all sounds great so far, but that's a lot of money and as I said earlier, it's too high for me to consider."*

You must now take them seriously because it has been said twice. If you ignore it this second time you may be out of the game.

You will now try to find out what their reason was for saying your price is too high.

Steps 1 to 3 for Overcoming a Price Objection

The initial Clarification part of the approach for a Pricing Objection will involve STEPS 1 to 3 of the answering objections process.

In most cases these first three steps will almost always be the same for any price objection.

Clarification

Step 1 - Questioning of the Objection

Step 2 - Listening to Their Answer

Step 3 - Repeating your Understanding of the Objection back to them.

Clarification Steps of a Price Objection

STEP 1 - QUESTION IT

You ask: "Could you explain why you feel our price is too high.

Do not fear what they will say, because it is the only way that you will be able to see why it is too much money, and if it is a real condition or just an objection.

After you have asked this question

STEP 2 - SHUT UP AND LISTEN!

Listen to their entire explanation.

Do not interrupt until they are finished unless it is clarification of a comment. We have already explained why it is important to hear them out.

Write down their Reasons

STEP 3 – CONFIRM THEIR ANSWER

Tell them your understanding of why they feel the price is too high

You say: "Thank you for explaining. If I understand correctly, your main reason(s) for saying the price is too high is (your understanding).

After telling them your understanding of why they feel the price is too high; if they agree, you will be dealing with their stated reason for the objection.

Solution Steps of a Price Objection

STEP 4 – ANSWER THEIR CONCERNS!

You will now take the appropriate steps to overcome the condition or objection and find the solution for them.

This is where your responses will differ. We have separated the main kinds of pricing objections into four types.

STEP 5 – CONFIRM YOUR ANSWER

Once you have provided your solution, you need to confirm that you have answered their concerns. If you have answered them, it is time to close.

The Four Types of Normal Price Objections

The following examples are the four main types or reasons for saying the price is too high.

We will outline the final approach that should be taken for the solution of each of them, separately.

Normal Price Objections

1. Over our Budget
2. We found Used for Less
3. We do not see the Value.
4. Higher than Competition

Normal Price Objections

Overview

The first three steps of the PRICE OBJECTION

Have been completed per our previous example

The Clarification Answer is "Over our Budget"

This is usually the result of not enough qualifying questions and you have been assuming everything is on track.

Your Present Position

You now need to determine if you can solve the situation dealing with price alone while you are there, or will you need to return to your office for a complete review.

This could also be a condition; but, we will treat it as an objection until proven otherwise.

Most purchasers will complain about price to get the best price they can for their company, as that is their job.

If they are insisting that your price is over their budgeted amount this possibly makes it a condition.

Before you go further, you will need to ask approximately how much you would need to lower the price, to achieve their budgeted amount.

The Solution Process

STEP 4 – ANSWER THEIR CONCERNS!

You ask: *"If we are able to resolve this price issue, will you be placing the business with our company?*

If they say YES keep going

If they say NO, you need to ask more questions until you get YES

Or find out why their answer was No

When you do get a Yes

Continue with: *"To deal with this properly I will need to know approximately how much over your budget we are talking about here."*

"Based on the figure that you give me; we will have two possible directions to take.

1. *If we are close, I will call the office for our best price."*

2. *If the price difference is too great, we will probably need to do a total review back at the office.*

Based on the Figure they give you

You will Know Which Direction you are Taking

Direction 1) Price is Close

You Say: *"I will now call the office and see what the best price is that we can offer, based on you making a decision today."*

Note: You should always leave some room to lower your price for any presentation to be prepared for this part.

You have now turned this into a close when you offered to call your office for your best price if the prospect places the business with you that day.

This way you can get the sale while you are there.

You have now called your manager (office) and asked them to do a quick review while you are in the prospect's office.

Note: This part should be only for show. You should already have made this review before you left your office for your final presentation. This way you already have your best Price available.

Make it for your offerings *"as-is"*

With No Changes.

This is a good procedure to follow on all reasonably sized orders and maybe leave some room to move in all the smaller ones as well.

Leaving room to move in any final presentation; to get an order, is a very good procedure to follow.

The reason why you never go in with your best price to start; is that, most purchasers feel you have room to move anyway, so do not let them down.

Play their game

The Set Up for the Close

Before you called your manager, you explained to your prospect what you are about to do.

You said: *"What I will do is call my manager and ask what our best price will be if we proceed with the order today. Does that sound fair?"*

The Key Phrase here is *"if we proceed with the order today"*

It justifies the Call while you are there

When they said "OK" you made the call

When you called your manager, you explained the situation even though you had pre-arranged the possible call. You stated the price that you are trying to get down to. (if available)

You said: *"If we can meet this price they will be placing the order with us today."*

You asked if they would do a quick review and you will call back in about 10 minutes to get their answer.

Note: Make this offer to call, even if you know you can probably meet the price. Do it in front of your prospect.

Even if you cannot meet the price stated, you have shown that you made the attempt and can now make a counter offer, without changing anything in your proposal.

Call your office back after the 10 – 15 minutes are up and pretend you are discussing the results of your request.

Say things like:

- "Yes, I know
- *We covered that*
- *They want to keep those benefits"*

Carry on and finish with: *"OK I will call you back before I leave."*

STEP 5 – CONFIRM YOUR ANSWER

You may be presenting what they want or making a counter offer. Whichever it is you will be confirming the results of the call you made to your office.

You Say: *"My manager has agreed to offer you everything with no changes for (state the price)*

SHUT UP!

Wait for an answer

This is a close

If they accept the price you say: *"Great Let's get started by changing the price on the proposal."*

You have just presented a closing statement and have an order if they say "Yes"

NOTE: We have just covered the approach for reviewing price only. This approach will work for any situation where the price is close.

Direction 2) Price Difference Too Great

We will deal with two types of proposals here

a) An offering with Accessories and/or Installation
b) An Offering without Accessories or Installation

STEP 4 – ANSWER THEIR CONCERNS

They have provided information that clearly shows that the price difference is too great and is beyond a simple price reduction.

We will outline your approach for two types of Large Projects.

a) A large system with many accessories or Installation.
b) A large System with no accessories or installation.

a) Large System with Many Accessories or Installation

It will be necessary to separate as many items from the main price and show them as options. You will then need to go back and review everything and prepare a new proposal.

You Say: *"It appears the difference is too great. You and I will need to review the proposal to remove as many items as possible to price separately as options, to see if we can get the price down."*

"We might even find some things that we are doing that you were planning to do, or our competition is not doing, and we will show them separately as well"

"We will then need to review our pricing to see if we can improve any areas and show these items priced separately as options for both of us to review on my next visit."

You Continue: *"That way you decide what stays and what goes once you see the numbers."*

"Is this an acceptable way for us to proceed?"

Wait for the Responses of your Client

If it is not a condition but an objection, and just an attempt to lower price, they may hesitate in eliminating features and benefits to get there.

Either way you will find out if it is a condition or objection by the time you finish this process.

- If it is a condition the next steps could solve the issue.
- If it is an objection the next steps will certainly test the waters and allow you to close.

If the Prospect Agrees

You Say: *" Let's see what we can separate to lower the price."*

You will now suggest eliminating items from the main price to show as optional items.

Explain that you will show separate prices for each option for them to pick and choose so they can get the cost down.

It will be like a summary question close; but here, you will separate items to show them as options.

This approach will mean gathering information and going back to the office for a review and some number crunching.

Begin a summary of components, features, installation responsibilities and items in your terms and conditions that could be options.

Often items such as electrical, plumbing or other civil work could be done by their own maintenance department instead of your crew and covered by their own overhead infrastructure.

As mentioned previously, you might even find out that your competition is not doing some items that you are.

You ask:

- *How about this item?*

- *How about this item?*

Continue through the entire list of items you know can be eliminated without affecting the overall integrity of what is needed.

When you are finished, you should have a substantial list of items to be eliminated or shown as options. If this happens, you will go back and review everything with your manager.

Say you will try to separate as many additional items as you can come up with, to price separately. Ask them to also think of what else they might want to see as an option.

Do not worry. This will happen when larger items or installation responsibilities need to be removed and priced separately.

The pricing exercise will be substantial, and you cannot resolve the matter when you are there.

Before you go back to begin your Review

- First you need to re-confirm how much too much you are. Even approximately will do at this point. You must have a target.

- In most cases, what they say will be lower than what they can live with.

- Secondly you must confirm that they will wait until you have time to review and can present a new offer with options for consideration.

- If they agree, arrange a new day and time for your next meeting before you leave.

Return to your office

- Remove the items to be shown as options

- Begin your price adjustments.

- Part of this review may involve your installation (what you do, and what they do) and maybe pricing or other terms and conditions.

- You will call the next morning following your meeting and see if they have thought of any more areas to be shown as options.

- Add their items (if any) and continue preparing your new proposal with as many options with separate prices.

Do not stop with what was discussed at the meeting and the results of your call the next day. Give the prospect as many options as you can.

b) An offering with no Accessories or Installation

We have just covered the approach for a large project that involves many items and Installation.

A similar approach will be taken for any *over-our-budget* situation where the price difference is too great to review while you are there.

The main difference will be the number of items to review or it could just mean re-working your numbers for your best offer possible.

It could be the type of offering where there is no installation or there is nothing tangible in the way of accessories to remove.

They say the price is still too high, the only thing you can do is offer to go back and review everything.

A large Price Reduction while you are there

Would not look good

If you did this, the prospect would possibly get angry as you were overpriced to start. Too much to review for an immediate answer regarding Price is not unusual.

STEP 5 – CONFIRM YOUR ANSWER

When you are finished all the reconstruction, return and present your new proposal.

Ask for the Order

CLOSE IT!

WITH THE APPROPRIATE CLOSE

2 - Used for Less

Overview

We will take the position that the Clarification STEPS 1 to 3 in your Answers to Objections procedure have been done.

The prospect has said (The have found "Used for less") is why they feel the price is too high. This means you possibly faced with a condition.   You will try to change it to a simple objection.

You will continue

Your client has shown interest and is saying the price is still over an amount they want to pay.

They say that you are the only one left offering new equipment that they are talking to, and they would like to have your product or service, but, they just cannot afford it.

Yes! It could be a Condition

But Initially treat it as an Objection.

If it is a condition, and you cannot overcome it; you can offer a leasing plan. Maybe it is time to consider lowering your price only as a last resort.

It is never good to do this unless you feel it is the only way to save the order.

Your final option is that you can pack up and go home.

But, first

- Doubt it as a Condition
- Acknowledge it as an Objection
- Begin Step 4 – Answer their Concerns

If it is an objection, it might turn out to be just more than they feel they want to pay for the product or your services.

The Solution Process

STEP 4 – ANSWER THEIR CONCERNS

Option 1 Call Office for Best Price.

You can call your office for a price reduction and proceed the same as we did for the previous example Reason 1 - "*It is over our Budget.*"

Make your Closing Attempt

If not Successful Proceed to Option 2

Option 2 Price Features Separately

Very often when comparing New and Used there will be value added features that the new equipment offers.

Offer to remove features that the other equipment does not have and show them as options, the same as we did for Reason 1 - "*It is over our Budget.*"

If the Prospect Agrees

Start the Separating Process

Follow the same procedure and come back with your revised offer. Make your Closing attempt to get the order.

If at this point they still feel the revised price is high and do not want to give up any of the options. The client is now being a little stubborn or ridiculous. Ridiculous or stubborn or both, you need to become a little ridiculous back.

We will now Treat it as an Objection

Our Example Situation:

Let's say the prospect needs a new lift truck to handle larger loads and their significantly increased material handling volumes. They are now on a two-shift basis, and the one truck they have is just not enough to handle the increased requirements.

Your truck is perfect because it is NEW and has everything the prospect wants.

- It has the extra load capacity they need.

- It can lift the height required in the new storage area.

- It also has a reach option for the maneuverability in their narrow aisles.

You are the last supplier of new trucks they are talking to. They like your truck

But they say: *"Your truck is just too expensive.*

A friend of theirs has a used truck they no longer need

Its Qualifications

- It is five years old; it has a greater load-lifting capacity than yours, and far more than they need.

- The higher load-lifting capacity makes the used lift truck larger in size and more difficult to maneuver in the small isles.

- This means they will need to wider Isles for turning and as a result they will end up with less storage capacity.

- It does not have the full height capability or the reach feature that your truck has which means the existing truck is required for the upper storage shelves.

- Your lowest price is now $5,000 more than their friend is asking for used, and you know you have now given your prospect your best price.

The items just listed emphasize your value-added selling features as well as the used truck's limitations. If this is not enough to convince your prospect, continue the process.

The Solution Process for our Example Situation

STEP 4 – ANSWER THEIR CONCERNS

You now say: *"I can understand how you feel; I agree that $ 5,000 is a lot of money."*

Have your Calculator Ready

Start the Process

Do this Exercise

Reduce the amount the client is objecting to, down to the absurd, and throw it back to them. It may be your only way left.

Money can usually be reduced to the lowest common denominator. The approach may change depending on what is too much, but this method can be very effective.

You already know that you are now $5,000 higher in price, so you state that as a known fact and go from there.

You say: *"You have said that we are $ 5,000 high, is that right.*

Once you have established this as your base you start the questions.

Ask the Questions and Know the answers already

You can also eliminate the questions and just keep going with just suppling the answers or **some of both**.

The question/answer process will involve them more and this is good; but, it could also annoy your client.

Choose the right Mixture to Suit the Situation

Begin the Questions

Question 1 - "How long do you want this truck to last?"
Answer 1) – They have already said ten years.

Question 2 - "How much is that per year averaged over ten years?"
Answer 2) their answer is $500.00 per year.

Question 3 - "How many days in a year are you in production?"
Answer 3) their answer is 240 days, or you provide it.

Question 4 - "How much is that a day?" Help them if they start to hesitate
Answer 4) you say: "I have my calculator. It is $ 2.08/day."

Question 5 - "How many hours do you work per day?"
Answer 5) the answer is 15 hours on an average day.

Question 6 - "That's how much an hour?"
Answer 6) the answer is 13.9 CENTS. Round it up to 14 cents.

You have just taken your client on a journey that has shown them how little they are talking about when it comes to the actual *time-of-use* cost.

STEP 5 – CONFIRM YOUR ANSWER

You now say: *"We have already established that:*

- *You have a ten-year life requirement*
- *You really need the lift height on the second truck as well, for the top row storage.*

- *You also need the reach to enjoy the narrow aisles and extra storage capability.*

- *You really do not need the higher load-lifting capacity because of the load limits on your storage racks.*

- *Our smaller truck size will make maneuverability possible in your narrow aisles giving you more storage."*

Ask: *"How much business might you lose in a year by sacrificing your needs for this lower price?"*

Wait for an Answer but you do not really need one

You just want them to think about it.

You now Say: *"We know our truck is new and will last ten years and it has everything you want and need for just 14 cents per working hour more."*

Ask: *"How long do you think the used truck will last before you experience repairs and extra maintenance costs?"*

Pause but - Once again no answer is really needed

If they are still Hesitating

Continue: *"How often could you experience an employee pay raise for such a low amount as 14 cents per hour?"*

"Would you not agree to it, if it meant keeping one of your key employees?

Pause - Once again no answer is really needed

Continue: *"By giving up height and reach you could also lose considerable time and storage capacity in making do - and as we stated earlier this will cause you to lose potential income and lower your profits."*

Pause - Once again no answer is really needed

Finish with: *"Is it not worth 14 cents an hour to have what you want and need, instead of settling for something that cannot do the total job?"*

Without looking extremely ridiculous

How can they now say that 14 cents an hour is too much to pay?

Leasing rates will make the hourly costs even more ridiculous.

Ask for the Order

CLOSE IT!

PRICE AND POOR PRESENTATIONS

Often you will have objections because you just did not make a good enough presentation to show your prospect the value-added features.

You may Not have asked enough qualifying questions

You may have failed in your presentation to show how your products or services provide benefits that will offer things like:

1. Additional savings, easier to operate, happier employees

2. Provide better quality of their finished product

3. Save time and energy and increase productivity.

Often companies have products that are far superior to some of their competition and this will probably be reflected in the price.

The biggest mistake that is often made; is that the sales person will assume that these features are self-evident, and do not need to be fully explained.

The prospect is viewing other suppliers and if there appears to be no additional benefits because of your higher price.

Their Choice Will Probably Be Price

Avoid this objection by improving your presentation and emphasize every benefit and feature; to the point where, there is no question in the prospects mind that the extra value is there.

Often you will need to make this review of value-added benefits or features; because the prospect needs a little more convincing, to tip the scales in your favour.

Poor Presentation Price Objections

1. We do not see the Value

2. Higher than Competition

1 - Cannot See the Value

Overview

The STEPS 1 to 3 in your Answers to Objections procedure has been done and they have said Reason 3 *"They do not see the value"* is why they feel the price is too high.

This response is an indication that you have not done a good enough job in presenting your offerings.

You have Failed to Establish Value

For future situations, you will need to review all your presentations and find what you need to do, to show value.

Often discovering the true objection will simply provide a doorway to use one of your other closes.

In this case, it is probably an overall review type closing. You must now try to fix your mistakes, while you are there.

The Solution Process

STEP 4 - ANSWER IT!

Your answer can be to do a Summary Question Style Close or Lost Sale approach. (*Shown in Part 2- Qualifying and Closing*)

The Close

You would take the following approach and apologize to your prospect. You should also be very embarrassed with the presentation you have just made.

You say: *"Obviously, I have done a very poor job in my presentation and for that I very much apologize."*

"If I had done a proper job you would not have this question of Value."

"Even though I know the value is there, I have done a very bad job of explaining the benefits of our product and where the value is for you."

"So that I do not make the same mistake again and perhaps discover what I did wrong here, do you have a quick few minutes to see where I went wrong?" I am sure you will also benefit if my previous presentation failed to show benefits you need and want."*

If they say: **"Sure or Yes"**

You say: *"Let's just do a quick review of the features and benefits of our products and services to see if we can find out where I failed to show the value.*

If the prospect feels they have missed something, they will probably want the review as well. Do not panic.

Make your review as a *Summary Question Close* and cover your features and benefits step by step. This time do a better job of demonstrating value.

You review and explain each feature and ask after each: *"Do you see the added value in this feature?*

Review and Ask: *"Do you see the extra value in that feature*

Keep going!

Continue through the entire description of your offerings until your questions produce a *"NO, I do not see the value here."*

At this point you stop and say: *"So that is where you do not see the value, is that right?*

Wait for an answer and say: *"I am truly sorry if I did not explain this well enough. What is it about (the item) that you do not see the value?"*

1. **Let them answer completely**
2. **Review the benefits and features and where the value is**

When you are finished your Review

You say something like: *"Can you now see that this feature has:*

Cut operating expenses,

Increased production capabilities

Will lower the rejection rates by considerable amounts

Continue: *"Were these not three of your greatest concerns."*

STEP 5 - CONFIRM THE ANSWER!

You say to the prospect: *"From what we have explained, have we provided everything that you have asked for and need?*

You now ask:*" Does our review answer your concerns on value or shall we continue our review further?"*

Continue your review until they say there are no more questions of value or you finish everything possible in your review.

You now ask: *"Do you feel that we have shown the value-added benefits and features, that you were after?"*

Wait for a YES

Finish by saying: *"I think you can you now see the value. Am I right?"*

If it solves the issue and they say

"They can now, see the value"

CLOSE IT

WITH THE APPROPRIATE CLOSE

2 - Higher Than Competition

Overview

The STEPS 1 to 3 in your Answers to Objections procedure have been done and they have said *"You are higher than your competition."*

Therefore, they feel the price is too high. This means you are faced with an objection.

Again, this is probably a presentation problem and a failure to show value over your competition.

You are possibly faced with someone who cuts corners or offers lower quality, poor service or does not meet all the prospects needs.

This objection comes from the prospects lack of understanding and seeing where your value-added features will create a far superior return on their investment.

Again, improving your presentation will greatly reduce these kinds of objections. This is where you might need to use more of your price rebuttals earlier in the process.

You will continue with STEP 4 and answer their concerns and then ask for the order

The Solution Process

STEP 4 – ANSWER THEIR CONCERNS

Stage 1

You have said that we are higher than our competition and I am not surprised by this comment.

We hear this on many occasions and it causes us great concern because too many people just look at price.

You say: *"Do you not agree that any company that provides products or services today has two directions they can take.*

1. *They can choose to provide a product or service that will give their customers everything that the client will possibly need and expect.*

Or

2. *Alternatively, they can do as little as possible and provide the least that they can get away with, so that their selling feature will be the best price?*

"Would you agree with those directional options?"

Unless the prospect is being ridiculous

The answer will be a yes.

Ask them: *"May I ask approximately how much higher we are?"*

The prospect should tell you the approximate difference. If they do give you a figure take whatever number, they give you and use it in your answer.

If they will not tell you; even approximately, and since they have said your competition is cheaper, you are now ***shadow boxing***.

It is not out of line to make the following statements about price vs. quality, benefits, performance etc.

- **Again, do not forget** the list of rebuttals you made to argue against price or the bad reasons for a lower price.
- It is alright to look a little concerned because they are about to waste your time with the shadow boxing.

If they do provide you with an answer regarding price carry on.

- Thank them
- Acknowledge the price and continue

The Turning Point

Of your Answer to this Objection

STEP 5 – CONFIRM YOUR ANSWER

Either way; with a price, or without a price, keep on the same pathway.

You say: *"Our Company does not cut corners to obtain the lowest price; but we are aware of others, who do."*

You continue: *"They will make their selling feature price, and not performance, or customer satisfaction because they know most purchasers are looking at price."*

Summary Questions you may ask

1. *"Would you not agree that doing as little as they can do for you, puts them in the best position to talk about price?"*
2. *"Which would you prefer Price or Performance?"*

3. *"What do you need this product or service to do for you?*

- *Everything you want and need,*

- *Or as little as the supplier you choose can get away with?"*

If they say, *"Everything I need and want"*

Ask for the Order

CLOSE IT

WITH THE APPROPRIATE CLOSE

Continue to practice ways to improve the message of value. This is primarily a presentation problem and one that happens all too often for sales people.

COMPETITION OBJECTIONS

Overview

You will almost never be without competition. I will not say that you will *"never"* have competition because on rare occasions; if you have serviced a client well enough, they will not seek competitive bids.

You have gained their complete trust and they know you will be fair.

Having a very good reputation and service record can also often place you in a preferred category when submitting a proposal as well. Here price is not always the main consideration, but it is still important.

These privileges must be earned and not abused. It is great when you are in either of the above two positions. Most often you are not, but it does happen.

On many presentations, you will be on the other end of things and will be up against the competitor with the preferred position. When this happens, you will often see the signs.

Do your research and look for a history that your competition might have with your prospect.

Most times you will have a relatively level playing field. We say relatively because often the person who makes the first best impression starts off with a slight advantage.

If it is you, then you must fight extra hard to stay there.

Marketing Advantage

The successful marketing of a company and its offerings will often make a big difference where one starts and can provide an initial advantage.

That is why having a good marketing plan is essential when creating a company image.

Good Branding of a company or offerings creates a comfort zone with the prospect right from the beginning, even before they begin conversations with the sales representatives.

The Company is Already Known

And Trusted by the Prospect

You will often find yourself competing against these types of companies. It is a challenge but not impossible to overcome.

A Starting position behind these companies can often be temporary if you present yourself, your company and offerings well enough. Many races are won by people coming from behind.

Become a Familiar Face

Companies will rarely buy from an unknown source or a stranger.

A very Important

Part of your job

Will be to become very Visible and Known

If you make one call as a stranger and return with a quotation and have had little or no interaction with the prospect in-between visits; you will most often, remain a stranger.

And find it difficult to get an Order

It is important to find ways to become a familiar face and well known. You need to become a comfortable source as a supplier. Find ways to accomplish this without becoming a pest.

Unethical Competition

You will often run into competition that does not play by any rules.

They will undermine you, your company and its offerings, to gain a better position for consideration of an order.

They will cut corners, provide inferior products to be able to present a lower price.

It will always be a challenge when this happens because often these things will go undetected by the client and you.

The below standard offerings are not seen by the prospect, and the mudslinging is not seen by you.

When you encounter an attitude change with a client, look for the cause and it will often be an unethical competitor.

Do not Become one of them

Defend yourself because it is your right to do so. Use your closes and answers to objections in an ethical way to outsmart them.

1 - Your Competition is Better

Overview

This is a common occurrence as branding, and a familiar visible image of a company or offerings will often be the cause.

There may be a history of business between the two companies or maybe a better presentation was made by them.

You must now challenge this statement and find a way to take over the primary position for the order.

The prospect says: *"Your competition has a better plan or a better product or service."*

- You should know your competition and what they offer, because that is your job.
- If your (product, service) has everything they have, or you are well positioned with other benefits or prices, you have a good chance.
- Do not argue.
- Do not challenge them with your knowledge at this point.

The Clarification Process

STEP 1) - QUESTION IT?

You say: *"Just to clarify what you are referring to, what is it that you feel our competition has, that we do not have?"*

"What makes them better?"

Your prospect might try and come up with something, draw a blank, or start providing you with several things.

STEP 2) - SHUT UP AND LISTEN!

- o Listen to the complete list.
- o Write the complete list down

When the prospect is finished

Then you say: *"Is that everything that you can think of at this point?"*

STEP 3 - CONFIRM THEIR ANSWER

Look and act extremely concerned and interested – *because you should be!* The prospect has just told you where and why they feel your competition is better.

If you know your product or service is equal or even better in some areas; you should be very excited, but also embarrassed at the same time because you did not cover these points well enough.

You say: *"So these are where you feel our competition is better."*

Wait for their *"Yes"*

"Are these areas holding you back from making a decision in our favor?"

LOOK EMBARRASED

I MEAN REALLY EMBARASSED

Because you should be

If you failed to point out your features the first time

Now you say: *"You know I am truly embarrassed that I did not make things clear enough. I am upset that I missed those features when I made my presentation and I am very sorry that I did not do a better job."*

Start Repeating the list they gave you

And say: *"Let's take a quick look"*

The Solution Process

STEP 4 - ANSWER THEIR CONCERN

"You say to them

- o "They have THIS" you reply – *"We also have that feature."*
- o "They have THIS" you reply – *"We also have that feature."*
- o "They have THIS" you reply – *"Whoops that is new one for them. I did not know they had that.   We also have it."*
- o *Here our features are much better. (explain why)*
- o *Here we have more benefits. (explain them)*

Build your list until you have totally overshadowed the competition with your features and benefits.

Answer the entire list

Then say: *"Can you think of anything else that you feel makes their product better, before I go on?"*

If they say: *"Yes"*
You ask: *"What is it?"*

Start making a list again if necessary. Carry on until they have nothing left.

STEP 5 - CONFIRM YOUR ANSWERS

You now say: *"So it looks like we have fully addressed your concerns about the competition being better.   Am I correct?"*

Ask for the Order!

CLOSE IT!

2 - Happy with Present Supplier

Overview

This will usually occur during your first meeting.

The prospect says: *"You know I have been working with "Bill's Plumbing" for over six years now, and I am really happy with their services."*

You say: *"I can fully appreciate that, (by pass it) by the way how long have you been in business?"*

They answer: *"15 years - but I am really happy with Bill as a supplier." (Second time mentioned)*

The Clarification Process

STEP 1 - QUESTION IT

You now continue: *"If you do not mind me asking, what brought you to start using Bill's services six years ago?"*

STEP 2 - SHUT UP AND LISTEN!

Hear your prospect out completely. Write any significant items down.

STEP 3 - CONFIRM THEIR ANSWER

Repeat their answers back

"So, what you are saying is that Bill had the best service, best prices and the greatest number of things that you wanted to see in a (plumbing service/supply company) at that time, six years ago."

They say: *"YES"*

CONFIRM IT! – *"So that is why you started using them?"*

The Solution Process

STEP 4 - ANSWER THEIR CONCERN

Wait for the answer and continue: *"I am sure that these things are still very important to you today – is, that right?*

Pause and continue with: *"I feel our products and service might be able to offer you equal and even have some additional benefits."*

"We have more service vehicles on the road, a much larger inventory to draw from, and we understand from our customers that we are extremely competitive in our prices."

5. CONFIRM YOUR ANSWER

Qualify his original reason for choosing Bill.

You say: *"Service, quality and price - Is that not what you are still looking for in a supplier?"*

Wait for the answer and it should be a "YES."

You continue: *"We can help you reconfirm that the same conditions still exist today with BILL as they did six years ago, by providing you with some pricing for products or services that you currently use?"*

"In this way, you will find out if the same situation holds true as it did 6 years ago?"

If the customer starts to object to the direction you are taking,

You say: *"I understand what you are thinking right now; but there is a real benefit in what I am proposing, and it is this."*

"If after doing this, we both find that the same circumstances still exist, and BILL still has the best of everything you need, your situation is reaffirmed, and we will have our answer and be on our way."

Continue with: *"If it **does not still exist,** I see two choices.*

The Choices

1) You can try to get better quality, better prices or services from BILL, (using us as someone wanting your business) and if you are successful then it's a win situation for you.

OR

2) You can give us a chance somewhere that does not mean switching over completely, and you get an opportunity to test us as a back-up to Bill, without damaging that relationship.

Does that sound like a fair approach?"

3 - Brand B is Better

We will look at two possible times when this situation might occur.

1) Your first meeting

2) At the end of your presentation

1) Your First Meeting

You have just introduced yourself and your company. You are just starting to explain your products and services.

You have not yet started to ask questions and the prospect decides to cut the meeting short and send you on your way. They may have changed their mind about seeing you.

It also could be that you did not Pre-Qualify the prospect well enough when introducing yourself and setting the appointment.

The prospect says: *"I did not realize what you were selling when we made the appointment and we use Brand "B". It's a great product and we are very happy with it."*

They continue: *"There is not much point in wasting your time because Brand "B" is better than anything I have previously looked at or used, so I am not really interested in looking at anything else!"*

Even though the prospect is trying to end the meeting; you did travel all the way to meet with them, and there may be a tiny bit of guilt feeling. If you get up and leave now, your trip is totally wasted.

The Clarification Process

STEP 1 - QUESTION IT

You now say: *"I apologize if I did not explain the reason for the meeting well enough"*

Pause for a second

Then continue: *"Could you take a quick few minutes to tell me, what it was that caused you to choose Brand B in the first place and what still makes it better?*

"This will really help my future knowledge if I run into Brand "B" again."

STEP 2 - SHUT UP AND LISTEN

At this point it looks like they have succeeded, and you are leaving. They will probably be more than happy to provide the reasons Brand B is better.

Their answer was that "Brand B" had more features and as they explain the features - you write them down. They had better service, better this, better that. They explained why, and you wrote that down.

Their prices were better. Keep listening and writing until they are done.

STEP 3 - CONFIRM THEIR ANSWER

You respond by saying: *"Thank you for taking the time to explain"*

Continue: *"So the reason was that, at the time you did your original survey, "Brand "B" had more of the things that you needed in a product than anyone else that you had talked too? Is that right?"*

Here is the Hook

A YES answer is almost guaranteed

They have just told you told you they were not interested because Brand "B" is the best. They have also just listed all the reasons why they like Brand "B" and are using it.

Can they now say NO?

When they say, "YES they had all the benefits"

You say: *"May I ask? Does the same situation still not exist today?"*

Wait for a response – It should be a *"Yes or What do you mean?"*

Continue: *"Are you not still looking for the product (service) that can offer you the most benefits to help your company also provide excellent service and better quality to your customers?"*

Repeat the list of benefits they gave you

"Would that not be something worth looking at again, even if it is just for reaffirmation that Brand B is still better?"

If their previous answer indicated that these things are why they chose brand B. Can they now say that they are not as important today as they were when they selected "Brand B"?

When they Confirm these areas are Still Important.

The Solution Process

STEP 4 - ANSWER THEIR CONCERNS

You say: *"While I am here we could select a few items and we will provide you with some prices and some product samples to try.*

*You can see if our products are equal in performance or perhaps - **what we hope for** - is that they might even be better than brand "B"*

"Is that a fair request?"

Wait for a response

Continue: *"If after doing this, we find that the same situation still exists, and brand "B" still has the best of everything you need, your situation is reaffirmed, and we will be on our way.*

If they have responded to your questions this far it will be very hard for them to say no without stating, they do not want what's best for their company.

STEP 5 - CONFIRM YOUR ANSWER

You continue: *"If brand "B" does not still have all of the reasons why they are the best, I see two choices available.*

1) You can try to get better quality, better prices or services from brand "B" using our products and prices as an example and if you are successful you have benefited."

OR

2) "You can give us a chance somewhere to act as a safety back up and supply a few of your needs as a secondary source."

"Does that sound fair?"

Get your required information. Come back with the samples for them to try. At the end of the trial period visit them again.

CLOSE THE SALE

---

2) At End of Your Presentation

You have done all your homework and it is your second or third visit. You have put together a final presentation that is based on the answers you got earlier on your first, second or additional visits.

Nothing was said indicating a strong loyalty to Brand "B".

You feel that you addressed everything that was outlined and came up with answers to all their questions and showed features and benefits that were equal to or better than your known competition.

You have supplied samples and/or provided items for a trial of your products and you saw that they were successful.

You have now just completed your final presentation and you know that you are competitive, and you have now asked for an order.

Your prospect has said: *"I have listened to your presentation and tried your products and we still feel Brand B is better."*

You now look, and act concerned and confused by their statement that "Brand B" is better. Your efforts have just demonstrated that you have equaled and, in some areas, surpassed the features they originally gave you for "Brand B". Your prices are also competitive.

It is time to get to the bottom of their feelings or you will leave without an order - so start your lost sale close approach.

The Clarification Process

STEP 1 - QUESTION IT

You say: *"It looks like we have not been able to convince you to use our product and I accept your decision and I am leaving."*

Close your briefcase or folder

And get up to leave and Stop.

And you say: *"I have obviously failed to show you all of the benefits of our products and where we offer some definite advantages".*

"Of course, I am disappointed."

Look disappointed and continue with*: "Just to help me understand why you still prefer Brand B; may I ask which area still makes you still feel that "Brand B" is still better."*

Stop and wait for an answer

If they do not give one

Do a summary Question Close!

You Ask:

- Was it their prices?

- Was it their service?

- Was it their features?

- Keep going until they indicate a reason

STEP 2 - SHUT UP AND LISTEN

Hear them out!   Your hope is that they will say something that will allow you to respond.

STEP 3 - CONFIRM THEIR ANSWER.

When they do make a response,

Repeat their answers back to them: *"So this (the reason) is why you still feel Brand B is better. Is, that right?*

The Solution Process

STEP 4 - ANSWER THEIR CONCERNS.

It is time to provide reasons why your product has met or even surpassed Brand B. You have now fully answered their concerns.

STEP 5 - CONFIRM YOUR ANSWER.

You now say: *"Now that should settle your concerns. Is, that right?"*

ASK FOR THE ORDER

If they are still not responsive

It's time for the Ben Franklin Close

Or time to leave as Promised

You have done everything now that you can to change their mind. Maybe they are buying from a friend or relative.

You cannot win them all, but it is your job to try – so thank them and leave the door open to come back and try again.

They are still a prospect and now they know you

TOMORROW IS ANOTHER DAY

CHANGE OF BASE

Overview

It is not unusual for a client to view things from a different perspective and miss an obvious situation.

They see one thing when they view your products or services and it prevents them realizing that you have already met all their needs.

Your job here is to show them the other way of looking at your proposal to realize that it really does fit their needs.

You simply change their way of thinking

You will

"CHANGE THE BASE!"

The Three examples:

1. Product is too Small

2. Product is too Big

3. You are too far away

1. Product is too Small

Overview

You have just made your presentation and you have met every requirement that you were given during your preparatory meetings. In some cases, you have gone beyond expectations.

The biggest mistake here is not making a smaller size a benefit or feature earlier in your presentation. It is now an issue possibly because your competition made it one or it is a normal reaction.

This is a "Change of Base Answer"

Size to Performance

The prospect has said: *"Your product is too small to do the job."*

The Clarification Process

STEP 1 - QUESTION IT

You ask: *"Why do you feel size will affect performance?*

STEP 2 - SHUT UP AND LISTEN

Listen to their answer.

STEP 3 - CONFIRM THEIR ANSWER

Repeat their answer back to them as you understand it.

You now reply: *"I understand how you could feel this way. Many other people have had this same reaction.*

The Solution Process

STEP 4 - ANSWER THEIR CONCERNS

May I ask; *is it not true that today, results are all measured by how well people or products do their respective jobs, not by their physical size?"*

Wait for their Answer

It should be: *"Yes that's true."*

You say: *"Yes, performance is the objective not size, and the modern manager of today gauges a person or a product's value by performance, not size.*

You continue: *"Is that not what we are talking about here? You are really interested in performance not size. Is that right?"*

They will have nowhere to go but say yes

Unless they are being ridiculous

STEP 5 - CONFIRM YOUR ANSWER

You say: *"You have tested our product and we both have seen that the results were more than satisfactory."*

"You have acknowledged that our price was more than competitive and yet we are discussing size as being a problem.

Continue: "You have also agreed that your main concern is will this product do the job that you want it to do? - Not how big it is? Isn't, that right?

Wait for their answer which should be a Yes

Ask for the Order!

CLOSE IT!

2. Product is too Big

Overview

You are dealing with a large piece of equipment here, or a large processing system.

You have just made your presentation and you have met every requirement that you were given during your preparatory meetings.

Your engineering department has calculated all the required measurements to ensure performance and product size capabilities and you know that you are not in an overkill situation regarding design.

The prospect has just said: *"Your product (System) is too BIG!"*

You know that your choice of materials and design allows you to build a very efficient product to fit into the smallest footprint possible.

The Clarification Process

STEP 1 - QUESTION IT.

You say: *"I am sure there is a reason why you are saying this and as I can see there are three possibilities here as to why you are saying our equipment is TOO BIG."*

You ask: *"Which one(s) would be correct?"*

1. *"You have reduced your part sizes or your specifications?"*
2. *"You have lowered the amount of floor space you have available?"*
3. *"We are too big compared to someone else."*

STEP 2 - SHUT UP AND LISTEN

You know that to handle the product sizes and specifications they originally stated, the equipment or footprint cannot be made any smaller without affecting their needs.

If the equipment is made smaller than you have proposed; it will mean cutting corners on design, sacrificing the integrity of your clients stated performance requirements, restricting the product size they can handle.

It might not meet code requirements which is not always evident. You also know your competition will do these things to get an order.

If #1 or #2 has changed

You will then ask to re-quote to adjust your size and price to suit. If nothing has changed in the part sizes, performance requirements or floor space, the only possible answer is.

It is TOO BIG when Compared to the Competition.

You have given them three choices and they have eliminated two of them.

This requires a "CHANGE OF BASE" Answer
Size to Price

STEP 3 - CONFIRM THEIR ANSWER

You say: *"You have now indicated that your part design or performance specifications have not changed."*

"You have also confirmed that you have not reduced the floor space available. But; You still say that our equipment is too big."

Continue: *"We know our equipment is not too big to fit the available floor space. The size is also needed to handle all the product specifications you requested, which also have not changed. It is also required to meet the industry code requirements.*

Conclusion by Elimination

You Say: *"It appears that we are too big compared to someone else, am I correct?"*

It is the only conclusion that makes sense and the customer will have to admit if it is so.

The Solution Process

STEP 4 - ANSWER THEIR CONCERNS

You Say: *"May we conclude that it is not just the size at issue here but probably PRICE as well?" Size usually affects price!"*

They will probably concede: *"It is PRICE."*

You know that your competition will undersize equipment or cut corners to obtain a lower price advantage. It often is done at the expense of the client.

STEP 5 - CONFIRM YOUR ANSWER

You now say: *"You have stated our equipment is too big on the premise that our competitor's size which is smaller can handle your requirements.*

Pause as if thinking then say: *"I think we may have an inferior design problem here that is the real issue."*

Continue: *"My further concern here is that if this assumption (size of the competitor offerings) is wrong, two things will happen:"*

1. *"WE WILL LOSE the order based on our own design integrity which is reflected in the increased dollar amount quoted."*

2. *"YOU WILL ALSO LOSE by not being able to handle all of your product sizes and meet the specifications that you have outlined in your performance criteria or satisfy the industry code requirements."*

You have effectively changed the BASE

From Size to Price

You have also brought design integrity into the picture.

You now might say: *"We often lose to price and it hurts. We also see that it is the client that suffers the most."*

"The sting of poor design and equipment performance painfully lives on – long after the initial joy of a lower price. The reality of inferior goods becomes a huge problem."

"It may be very costly to fix or even worse – it is not possible to fix."

"Unfortunately for us we must stand on our design integrity rather than provide a flawed system to obtain a lower price to get the order."

The final Questions

It is now time to ask the closing question using the alternative of choice:

You Say: *"Which is most important to you - a lower price today or getting the product you expected that meets all of your needs from now on?"*

SHUT UP AND WAIT FOR

"MEET MY NEEDS."

FINISH THE CLOSE

87

FINISH THE CLOSE

3. Location - You are too far away

Example Overview

You have just quoted to supply equipment worth $2,465,000.00 and you are there to get the order.

The prospect says that they like your proposal and that it has everything that they want but they have decided that you are just too far away to provide the service they need.

If you were closer, they would be very interested and probably give you the order.

This is a "CHANGE OF BASE" Answer

Distance to Time

Sample Locations for our Discussion

> The prospect is in Toronto, Ontario
>
> Your business location is Chicago USA - 708K or 440 miles
>
> Your competition is in Hamilton, Ontario – 73K or 45 miles

The Clarification Process

This is where you need to change the base of measurement from distance to time to show the prospect that you can provide the same service and possibly even quicker.

You have already done your research earlier and know who you are up against and where everyone is located distance and time.

STEP 1 - QUESTION IT

You say: *"Why do you feel that Distance is the problem?"*

STEP 2 - SHUT UP AND LISTEN

Here them out completely.

STEP 3 – CONFIRM THEIR ANSWER

You say: *"I can see why you might feel that we are too far away to service your account."*

You now say: *"May I just quickly review what you have said?* *"You like everything about our proposal except that you feel we are too far away?"*

"If wasn't for the "too far thing", we would be doing business with you today, is that right?"

When they say: "YES" You Begin…

The Solution Process

STEP 4 - ANSWER THEIR CONCERNS

You say, *"At first glance, I might also be just as concerned if I were in your position."*

You say: *"I see that you are comparing distances as your base for measuring service capabilities." "Am I correct in saying that distance and serviceability is your concern?"*

Your job now is to change the way they are measuring your company's ability to provide service. To do this, you need to change the basis of their thinking.

Wait for their acknowledgment and Continue.

You say: *"If you will allow me to provide a different viewpoint we might already have an answer to your concerns."*

You now Ask and Answer this way

You do not need to ask every question and wait for an answer. It might be better to just provide the answers yourself in certain areas.

Find the right balance and begin

You Ask: "How far is Hamilton from here?"

You know the Answer: "73 k or about 45 miles"

You Ask: "How much is that in time?"

**You know the Answer*: "70-80 minutes by car on a good traffic day"*

You Ask. "How far away is Chicago?"

**You know the Answer*: "708 k or about 440 miles"*

You Ask: "How much is that in time?"

You know the Answer:*" 65 minutes by plane plus 15 - 20 minutes by taxi - 80 – 85 minutes"*

You continue: *"Is it not true that in the global business world that exists today, that we no longer measure things by distance, we measure them by time?"*

"Is that, not right?"

Wait for their answer and it should be a "YES."

STEP 5 - CONFIRM YOUR ANSWER

You Say: *"So what you are really concerned about is the time that it takes to service your business not the distance involved."*

|Is, that Right?"

Wait for their answer again and it should be a "YES."

You continue: *"That is how we measure things today "Time – not Distance?"*

The only Reasonable Answer is "YES"

Then you say: *"So that should completely settle the service because of distance concern. Is, that right?"*

They will probably agree in most cases

It's time to ask for the order

CLOSE IT

They might say: *"What about Flight Delays"*

You Answer: *"What about Traffic Tie-ups"*

This cat and mouse list could go on and usually there will be a rebuttal for every concern presented.

In the End

If they still are opposed to the distance thing there is another answer that is a great follow up.

It is called – What Would You Do?

It is Next!

WHAT WOULD YOU DO?

This answer usually deals with what has been presented by the client as a Condition and usually conditions cannot be solved.

However, not everything that is presented as a condition; is one or must remain as one. We have learned earlier that all conditions should be challenged.

We have here three examples

What would you do?" Conditions"

1. No Service Close by

2. Objectionable Employees

3. Reputation of Product

There will be others that fall into this group. We are providing these three examples to enable you to follow the same conceptual outline to reach your goal.

1. No Service Close by

Overview

You have just made your presentation and made several attempts to close. You have answered all their objections and they are splitting hairs over your last answer to their objection.

Time not Distance

They still feel that because you are in Chicago that you will not be able to service them properly.

They empathize with what you are saying about time not distance being the measurement but have presented a counter argument about satisfactory flight times and airport delays, and perhaps several additional reasons.

It may be Stubbornness

Or a Legitimate Concern for their Hesitation.

If local servicing is an ongoing problem and your company wants to sell their products in distance related situations – no local service – is something that you will need to solve anyway.

Your company will need to find a local service company for emergency time sensitive service requirements.

You can still offer ongoing troubleshooting and training with your own people in Chicago.

Once you have corrected this situation

You will not lose orders because of this distance condition

The Clarification Process

STEP 1 - QUESTION THEM

You now say to them: *"Have you ever been in situations where you have missed opportunities time after time because you have not been able to satisfy your customers comfort zone?"*

"You have met everything that your prospect is looking for - except for this one area. "In this case, it is Distance"

STEP 2 - SHUT UP AND LISTEN

They can say either: *"Yes or No"*

How they answer does not really matter

STEP3 - CONFIRM THEIR ANSWER

You continue: *I understand your concerns about our ability to service even using time not distance as a measuring point."*

"It is a very legitimate concern when entering into a project of this size."

"It is our ability to look after you in a timely manner that is causing you to hesitate to place your business with our company – right?

"Servicing capability not product is we are talking about here. You feel that Chicago is just too far out of your comfort zone to be able to service equipment in the Toronto are. – Is, that right?"

Pause

"May I ask what you would do if something like this distance thing kept reoccurring with you and preventing sales?"

They will probably respond by saying that they would find a way to provide the required service locally.

If they do not say it, you say it

The Solution Process

STEP 4 - ANSWER THEIR CONCERNS

You say: *"That's what we are doing."* OR *"That's what we have done".*

You then say: *"We have retained a quality service company in your city that is familiar with our products for just this reason."*

 "They will be available on 24 hour 7 days a week basis to respond to time sensitive emergency requirements."

Optional; but if True, use it

"We are strong believers in using local installers whenever we can. We are doing this here. Since they are involved and working with us in the installation of your system, they will already be familiar with everything."

"They are more than qualified and will be providing our 24/7 service.

STEP 5 - CONFIRM YOUR ANSWER

You now say: *"As you can see we will be able to resolve an emergency requirement locally with local people. They will be able to obtain our input by telephone or internet connection if required."*

"As well, we can still provide our normal in-house assistance and trouble shooting from Chicago on a 24/7 basis."

"We also will still provide in person service calls, when required. You will be very well taken care of for service. Would you agree that this is a correct statement?"

Wait for their answer

It will almost be a guaranteed YES

CLOSE IT!

2. People Problems

Overview

This objection can happen at any time. It can also happen to anyone. It could be during your first call, during or at the end of your presentation or anywhere in between.

Things are going smoothly

And Suddenly this Objection is Made

Your prospect says: *"I remember now, I had someone call on me from your firm two years ago and they really upset me and several of my employees. Because of this, I will never do business with your firm again."*

The Clarification Process

STEP 1 - QUESTION IT

You reply: *"I understand how you feel." "Do you recall the name?"*

Pause briefly for a name but one is not really required

Continue: *"I think I know who you are referring to." Tell me; have you ever had one of your employees upset a customer in their actions or words so badly that the customer stopped giving you their business?"*

"You also discovered that this was happening with other customers and they were starting to reduce their business or even end their business with your company as well?

STEP 2 - SHUT UP AND LISTEN

If the prospect says: *"YES"*

You ask: *"What did you do?"*

If it has not happened to your prospect,

You say: *"Tell me, what would you do if that happened to you?"*

Hear them out. There are only a couple of directions they can go, but do not assume. Listen to their entire answer.

STEP 3 - CONFIRM THEIR ANSWER

Their answer will most likely be something that most people would do. They could say we fired that person, removed them from customer contact or severely reprimanded them.

No matter what they say

Repeat their solution back to them

The Solution Process

STEP 4 - ANSWER THEIR CONCERNS

You have placed them in your shoes and made them vulnerable to experiencing the same problem that they are objecting to.

You have asked for advice and they have provided an answer.

You say: *"That's what we did"*

You have shown them that you did exactly what they said they would do, to solve this issue.

Can they now object to doing business with your company when you have taken a course of action endorsed by them?

STEP 5 - CONFIRM YOUR ANSWER

Make sure the person is gone or is far enough removed so they will not have any contact with your prospect, if they are still with you.

If they are still employed with your company, indicate what strong definitive action was taken to remove the problem.

It could be something like: *"You know we discovered this was happening and this person was just not good with handling customers.*

Continue: *"We discovered they were great in other areas of responsibility completely away from customer involvement. We moved them to that position."*

"They are completely out of the equation."

You say: *"It seems we think alike, and our company has done the right thing to remove this problem, would you not agree?"*

Ask for an Opportunity to Quote

Or

If you have already quoted

Ask for the Order

CLOSE IT!

3. Product Reputation

Overview

You have previously made your attempt to set up an appointment, and you were successful in getting one.

You are now there to do your first presentation and you are suddenly met with this objection.

Your prospect says: *"Now I remember your company. I tried your products three years ago and they just did not work out for me."*

"The quality was just not there, we experienced failure after failure, and problem after problem."

"So, tell me, why should I even consider talking to you let alone taking another chance with your company?"

The Clarification Process

STEP 1 - QUESTION IT

This is the same type as the People objection.

You say: *"I definitely agree with your thinking and position?*

Pause for a second and continue: *"May I ask* if *you ever have a product that just did not do what you expected it to do?"*

"It was being returned and damaging your business and you were losing customers because of it?"

Like the first two examples you are not challenging the prospect. You are agreeing with them and engaging them in an empathetic dialogue.

You now say: *"What did you do?"* - Wait for the answer

If it has not happened to your prospect

You say: *"What would you do if this happened to you?"*

STEP 2 - SHUT UP AND LISTEN

They will either tell you what they did or what they would do.

STEP 3 - CONFIRM THEIR ANSWER

Whatever their answer is, you continue and repeat their answer back to them. If they have had the same experience or just told you what they would do continue with the next statement.

The Solution Process

STEP 4 - ANSWER THEIR CONCERNS

You say: *"That's what we did."*

"We discovered that we needed a better product line for our number one line and found a new one to replace the one we were having problems with as our main product line."

"The other older line has a place in certain areas and performs very well there. We also still needed to service customers who were using it successfully."

"We have it available for several very specific uses where it performs well."

"We will be offering our new product line to you. It has a proven track record."

Make sure you have the Alternative Offerings

STEP 5 - CONFIRM YOUR ANSWER

You Say: *"So it seems that we have taken your advice and I think you will see that the bad situation no longer exists. Does that remove your concerns?"*

You are now able to continue with your presentation. You have successfully removed the problems stated by them with the same advice they have provided.

Not only have you demonstrated that you fixed the problem; but you also did not abandon existing customers who were happy with the older product line.

Clarification

There are many ways to present your correction for this situation; but make sure you have replaced this product as your #1 offering totally with a better alternative or are not using the old product for this prospect.

If you have a product or service that has caused problems, this situation has probably come up many times.

Corrective Action is the only way to remove this ongoing objection and any responsible company who wishes to survive will take the steps as we have mentioned.

If corrective action has not been taken, then this approach is not appropriate.

If a new product has been introduced, then you can do the following at the end of the solution Process.

GET A REQUEST TO QUOTE

Or If You Have Already Quoted

Ask for the Order

CLOSE IT!

CONDITIONAL OBJECTIONS

Overview

The next three examples are very common occurrences in the selling process. Most often they are conditions that exist.

Sometimes you may be able to create an answer that will change it to a simple objection.

You will then take Steps

To Overcome the Objection

To Obtain the Sale

Often, they may be time sensitive or require changes, and you will be faced with a call back and final presentation when the condition has been met.

That means that when you hear one of these conditions you do not immediately pack your bags and leave.

You must try your best to resolve the condition while understanding it will probably remain a condition for a while longer.

Knowing how to remain in the game is essential when this type of situation occurs.

The THREE Condition Examples

1. I need to talk to someone
2. I am waiting for another Price
3. I want to Think It Over

1 - I Need to Talk to Someone

Condition 1 Overview

The prospect has participated throughout the entire presentation with you, with questions and objections, and you have answered all of them successfully.

You have made your Final Close

The prospect says out of the blue: *"You know I like everything I hear and see. You have answered all of my questions and objections to my satisfaction, but, there is one more thing I have to do."*

Here is the Condition

They Continue: *"You see (my Aunt Jenny) has been a longtime confidant and mentor for me, and before I make a decision like this, I like to discuss it with her and get her opinion."*

This one is a zinger that can really catch you off guard. Their mentor could also be the father, mother, spouse, son or daughter and they are almost always

Someplace Else

The Clarification Process

a) Change it to an Objection

STEP 1 - QUESTION IT

Stay calm and do not get upset.

Start by saying: *"From the results of our presentation, can I say that you are completely happy with everything that we have proposed here today?"*

STEP 2 - SHUT UP AND LISTEN

The prospect says: *"Yes that is correct."*

They explain that this is a procedure that has been ongoing for years.

The prospect has now created a roadblock that they feel has isolated them from any further attempts to close.

At this moment, they have created a condition and it is up to you to try to remove it or change it to a simple objection.

STEP 3 - CONFIRM THEIR ANSWER

You now say: *"So the main reason you cannot move forward today is that you want to talk to your Aunt Jenny about this, to get her input, her blessing, the rubber stamp, so to speak; before you move on with this project."*

"Is, that right?"

The client is happy with this question because it reinforces the condition and they are confident that you cannot go any further.

The Solution Process

STEP 4 - ANSWER THEIR CONCERNS

At this point you have confirmed their reason for not continuing any further until they speak with Aunt Jenny.

You will now begin to break down that defense with the following approach.

You Ask: *"Where is Aunt Jenny at this moment?"*

Find out where the person is and how they usually communicate, and if they are in another town or country.

Once you have established where they are and how they communicate in these matters respond accordingly.

If they are in a time zone where you can call now

You say: *"Would it make sense to contact your Aunt Jenny right now?*

Continue with*: "You can speak to her and explain what you are about to do, and that you would like her input and her blessing."*

I can step out of your office to allow privacy.

Continue *"In this way, I will be present to answer any questions that might arise, and if she feels it is a good idea, we can then proceed without any loss of time?"*

"If more discussion is needed then I can answer any immediate questions and make myself available if more should arrive later. Does that make any sense at all here?"

If they can be reached and your prospect will make the telephone call, answer any objections that might arise.

If it turns out the mentor is close by offer to wait or even accompany them and visit Aunt Jenny.

If they agree have the telephone call or meeting

THEN CLOSE IT!

b) The Condition Remains - Unable to Talk to Aunt Jenny

If the prospect does not agree with your suggestion, or if Aunt Jenny cannot be reached now.

You are faced with a Condition

It is time to step back and plan a CALL BACK.

After your attempt to solve it; your immediate suggestion for the call back may also cause them to be a little angry, so do not apply too much pressure.

You say: *"I can see that this is very important to you, and part of your process in these matters, so we can take one of two directions*

Direction 1- *We can establish a time when this discussion with your aunt Jenny can take place and I can make myself available by telephone or in person, to answer her questions."*

Or

Direction 2 - *"We could establish a time to get together after you have had a chance to discuss this with your Aunt Jenny."*

Finish with: *"Again, whatever makes sense for you is fine with me."*

At this point you have done everything possible that you can do. The need to talk to someone may be

- A legitimate reason
- A great objection
- A great opportunity for them to buy some thinking time

- An opportunity to talk to your competition

- A way to make it easier to say no when you make your next closing attempt.

The pressure is now off them and when you make the call back appointment - it will be DO or DIE!

A CALL BACK PRESENTATION

2 - Waiting for Another Price

Condition 2 Overview

This is a very common occurrence because not everyone can be the last one in. On the first call or during information gathering calls are times when you need to start to worry about positioning yourself.

Try to make an initial presentation or a preliminary offering that is done before preparing your final quotation. It is your dress Rehearsal as we call it. This is when the final positioning starts to become an extremely important factor.

The closer you are to last one in, the more information you will be able to obtain, to see where you are positioned regarding client preference.

If you know there will be another round, this is when you will make your efforts to be the last one in to avoid this condition. Everyone is now maneuvering to achieve the same thing and there are many tactics used to be last in.

The prospects choice of final positioning can sometimes indicate the order of their preference (saving the best for last), but not always.

No matter what the circumstances are; you will often find yourself facing this condition, and it is a difficult one.

Your prospect says: *"I am waiting for another proposal to come in." Or I am waiting for several proposals to come in."*

Again, stay calm and do not get angry.

You say: *"That's fine I understand."*

The Clarification Process

STEP 1 - QUESTION IT

You Say: *"I am sure you know that being the final presenter is what every sales person wants."*

"Would you agree with that comment?"

Continue: *"Someone has to be first or second, and it looks I have made my presentation earlier than others. The only questions that I might ask right now are these."*

"Do you have any concerns now with our company?"

"Do you have any concerns with our product?"

"Our delivery or Our price?"

You continue: *"May I also ask that, once you have listened to all of the proposals, if I might have the opportunity to talk with you before you make your final decision?"*

STEP 2 - SHUT UP AND LISTEN

The prospect will usually respond to your questions and usually will explain the situation; but, the condition will remain.

STEP 3 - CONFIRM THEIR ANSWER

You say: *"I understand and appreciate why you are still waiting for other quotations to come in. Making any kind of decision is premature at this point."*

The Solution Process

STEP 4 - ANSWER THEIR CONCERNS

You Say: *"I am sure you would agree that our promptness has made it more difficult to keep ourselves current with any changes that might occur."*

Wait for an answer

You Say: *"Often new conditions or questions arise after listening to everyone, and our existing quotation could no longer follow your new parameters."*

"That is why being first or second is difficult, because one cannot react to these changes."

STEP 5 - CONFIRM YOUR ANSWER

You ask: *"I fully agree that you will need to see all of the quotations before you can make a proper evaluation.*

Establishing the Call Back

You Ask: *"When do you expect that you will have seen all of the proposals, and will have had sufficient time to review them?"*

Wait for the answer

Continue: *"Can we establish a time to meet before I leave today?"*

This will probably not be possible at this point and it may appear to be rushing your client. Try anyway.

It may also be better for your chances; to arrange when to call, to arrange the appointment.

You ask: *"May I call you to set up a meeting (whenever they have said), so that I can answer any new questions you may have or make any adjustments before having our meeting?"*

If your prospect says: "YES"

Set the time for your meeting

YOU ARE NOW DOING

A CALL BACK PRESENTATION

3 - I'll Think It Over

This is the one that stops most sales people in their tracks. The sales person has just finished the final part of the presentation and has asked for the order. It can also happen just before they can ask for the order:

The prospect says*: "Thank you for a great presentation."*

"You know, I like what I see, you have done a great job of explaining everything; but you know I just really need to think it over. Give me a couple of days, and I'll call you."

This is often because of the natural habit of procrastination

Some people just resist doing things right away

They have indicated they like your product or service but need to think it over. Maybe there are some areas that are causing concern as well. If you leave now they will go unanswered.

The prospect may also be chuckling because **"I'll think it over"** usually stops most sales people from going any further.

The prospect knows that if they do not have to decide today, they are off the hook.

Their attitude is often: *"If they (meaning you) want the order let them work for it. They will come back. Who knows maybe I can get a better deal from them or someone else. Let them sweat a bit."*

Here is Where you can Change the Direction.

You say: *"Thank you for your kind words and appreciation of our presentation. I understand, and there is a lot to consider."*

"I can see that we have truly sparked your interest, or you would not be taking the time to think it over unless you were really interested. - Is that right?

They will almost certainly say: *"YES"*

They feel they have stopped your attempts to get an order and you are leaving.

By adding this next question, you change the entire game. You are now going to try and make them squirm a bit.

You continue and say: *"I can see that you are very interested and like what we have presented. I hope you are not just saying you want to think it over - just to get rid of me?"*

This question has a way of making the customer qualify their interest and tell you that they have not been wasting your time.

It has a way of turning things around and now they are on the spot.

Wait for the: *"No that is not it!   I am very interested, and I am not just wasting your time. I really do want to think about it."*

You now have them trying to justify the delay and they will usually emphasize that they really do want to think it over.

You then continue: *"You know I have found when people want to think things over, it is usually because they have some concerns, or something is unclear."*

"Just to clarify my own thinking, what part is it that is unclear, and you want to think over?"

Here the Approach is Different

Pause and wait for an answer - If they do not have one –

Do a Summary Close

THE CALL BACK OBJECTION

Overview

No one likes the idea of a call back especially if an appointment needs to be set.

If it comes out of a genuine reason why the prospect could not decide at the time you made your first presentation, ask for a time to get together while you are still there.

If they did not agree at the time of the condition, you must now set the date and do your presentation again.

We will offer four different reasons for the call back

1. You simply needed to review and revise your proposal
2. They needed to talk to someone who was not available.
3. They were waiting for other prices to come in.
4. They needed to think it over

If no appointment was scheduled and only an approximate date to call was made; follow the next steps.

Call to set the Appointment

We are giving Four examples for a Call Back

 # 1 - You say: "When we last talked, we spoke about getting together this week once I finished my revised proposal; which I have now completed.

 # 2 - You say: "When we last talked, we spoke about getting together this week once; you had a chance to speak with your Aunt Jenny.

 # 3 - You say: "When we last talked, we spoke about getting together this week; once you had received and reviewed all of the proposals.

 # 4 – You Say: "When we last met you needed time to think things over.

Continue: *"Have there been any new developments or changes that I might need to look at or consider before I come in?"*

Get the details if any, and make the changes needed to your proposal.

Very often, getting back in is a very difficult process; and this is when you will be met with the objection to the call back.

Do not ask "IF" you can come in

You ask, "WHEN" you can come in

You ask: *"Which day is best to come in - morning or afternoon. - 2:00PM or is 3:00 better.*

Wait for confirmation

Make your Call

And Presentation

CLOSE IT

Objection to a Call Back

No Need at Customer's Request

Your prospect answers your question about new developments in this way

They say *"No - I think we have all of the information we need to make our decision without the need for you to come in."*

This is usually an indication that you are not first in line for the order and maybe not even in the finals. It usually indicates that you need to get back in or it's probably over.

You will need to re-position yourself if you want a chance to get the order. It is time to dangle a carrot to see if they bite.

The Clarification Process

STEP 1 – QUESTION THEIR RESPONSE

You ask: *"Why have things changed about our coming in to*

- o *"Present our revised proposal."*

- o *"Discuss what your Ant Jenny had to say*

- o *"Review our proposal and discuss any changes we might need to make now that you have all of your proposals.*

- o *"Had a chance to think things over"*

STEP 2 - SHUT UP AND LISTEN

Listen to their explanation and ask any questions for clarification; but hear them out completely.

STEP 3 - CONFIRM THEIR ANSWER

Whatever their answer is repeat it back to them.

The Solution Process

STEP 4 – ANSWER THEIR REASON

You say: *"I understand what you have just told me, but in consideration of:*

- o   *Previous discussion when I was there*

- o   *The extra benefits and better price we now offer*

- o   *Or any other appropriate reason…*

We certainly would appreciate the opportunity to talk with you.

Do you not have 15 – 20 minutes on the day we originally set aside to review our proposal?"

Continue: *"During the last few days, last week (whatever it has been), we have made some significant improvements to our proposal. I think that it makes a big difference in how you would view our (products, system, equipment, or services)."*

The Chances

If you are in the top two or three being considered, the client will usually agree to see you to avoid eliminating a better offer resulting from your revisions.

STEP 5 - CONFIRM YOUR ANSWER

You Ask: *"Can we set a time to get together?"*

If they say: *"YES"*

Thank them, set and confirm the appointment time. Take the time to review and make your changes sizzle.

Make your Call and Presentation

Ask for the Order Again

CLOSE IT

No Appointment Possible

If they say *"NO"* to your request for an appointment - Do not get angry.

You simply say: *"Since I was already going to be in the area that day anyway, I would like to drop off the revisions so that you will have our latest proposal for consideration or at least have it on record?*

"I will just leave it at the front desk."

You say: *"Thank you for the opportunity. I will drop off the information* (name the day)."

The Follow up

Call the client the day you drop off your changes to see if they got them, if they have questions and where you now stand?

It is obvious that someone else has the advantage position. This happens.

Tell them you will call back in a couple of days to see if they have any questions. When the two days are up, it is time to make your call.

You ask again: *"Would you have time this week or next week to discuss our proposal?*

If they say yes, you are back in the game. Set your appointment time, make your presentation and ask for the order.

If they say No,

There is always Another Prospect

And another day

MUDSLINGING

We felt this topic was worthy of some discussion. Unfortunately, there will usually be competition engaged in this negative activity.

This is a tactic that many sales people use to try and position their company to get the order. It is not a good tactic to use as it can often backfire on the person doing it.

It is Bad Selling Tactics and Not Ethical

If your competition is bad mouthing you, think of it as being a good sign. Your competition has shown that they fear you and/or your company and cannot compete on a normal basis.

Do not respond with the same mudslinging methods. Just like Hockey; it is usually the last person into the fight, that is sure to get the penalty.

In this case, the penalty might mean elimination from any kind of consideration.

If the customer starts saying that they have heard things about your company or product that concerns them, even; if they are wrong, do not get angry or argue.

Hear them out

In many cases the prospect will be testing your integrity; to see if you have any, so do not retaliate.

Another Sign to watch for

You could also notice a sudden or significant change in the prospects attitude or involvement with you.

This could also be a result of mudslinging. Whether it is stated or suspected you need to defend yourself.

In either case

NEVER bad mouth a competitor or their product – just out-sell them.

The minute you lower yourself to the level of mudslinging, you have lost the right for the respect of your potential customer.

The prospect will now find it harder to buy from you, as negativity generates negativity.

Knowing which competitors engage in these negative mudslinging comments will give you the opportunity to use different approaches.

Make it part of your Presentations

You can say: *"We know that some of our competitors engage in mudslinging. We do not believe or get involved in this type of practice."*

"We also know that it is just their way of trying to level the playing field because they are intimidated by the higher quality and benefits of what we offer."

"They often try to remove us from quoting or a position of consideration this way."

> *"If you have some information about us that concerns you, all we ask is that we have the opportunity to respond."*

> *"We are not asking for names, just what has been said."*

> *"We do not want to do battle with them."*

> *"We do however wish to defend ourselves, which we have a right to do."*

If your prospect indicates that they have heard some negative comments

Treat it as an Objection

Handle it the Same Way

The Clarification Process

You should respond with this: *"Could we get your concerns on the table right now, so we can answer them?"*

> Listen to the comments.

> Repeat them back to the client.

The Solution Process

> Respond to them and defend yourself and your company.

When you have finished, you ask: *"Does that settle your concerns?"*

If No Cooperation

If they will not tell you what it is that they have heard, it is not good.

All you can say now is: *"There are always two sides to every situation."*

"And of course, our competition is not favoring our side"

You Continue: *"It is hard to shadow box with the unknown, and it is almost impossible to defend accusations you cannot hear."*

"May I ask if these factors will have had any effect on our ability to get this order?"

If they say: *"NO"*

All you can say is: *"Are there any other areas that you need answers to, or have concerns about, in what we have proposed?"*

If they say they have no other concerns,

ASK FOR THE ORDER

Mudslinging is a poor way to win orders and if the customer is not forthcoming with information, there is little you can do. Just do the best you can and that is all you can do.

As shown it is possible to still get the order if you ask the right questions. Do not return the mudslinging!

Remember the – *"What would you do"* approach discussed earlier and perhaps use it now."

Put them in Your Shoes

And ask

What would you do?

Wayne E Shillum - Author

View our other sales and marketing eBooks at

www.wesmarketing.com

SUMMARY

The Answers to objections that we have presented are not meant to trick your prospect. They are meant find out why they are hesitating.

Pressure without answering their concerns first, will only damage your reputation and that of your company.

Pressure after an unanswered objection, will only make clients angry.

The power of; how to find the cause for the objection, and being able to answer it, will give you all the ammunition that you will need from start to finish.

We have provided some basic ways to solve objections. In them, you will find the ability to combine different aspects from each to create new ways to answer objections and find solutions.

- Always treat objections as good things

- Do not fear them

- They are Buying signals that can lead you to the Order

From the first call to completion of the process and the final close; your efforts should be to build respect, trust and create a good relationship.

The best finish is getting the sale, the right way

- Avoid the Use of Bad words

- Do not become a Mudslinger

ALWAYS USE

THE FIVE STEP PROCESS

TO OVERCOME OBJECTIONS AND CONDITIONS

END OF PART THREE